CUSTOMIZE WALL STREET

A PRACTICAL GUIDE
TO STRESS-FREE SAVING & INVESTING

CUSTOMIZE WALL STREET

A PRACTICAL GUIDE
TO STRESS-FREE SAVING & INVESTING

HARVEY NEIMAN

MAJOR PRESS

Published by Major Press

Cover and Interior Book Design by Monkey C Media www.monkeycmedia.com

Edited by Jared Kuritz and Shelley Chung

Printed in the United States of America

ISBN: 978-0-9860871-0-3

Library of Congress Case Number: 1-1212956371

To Linda Neiman
My dear wife, you lost your battle for life before your time,
but you never lost my love. You stood by me, with strength
and devotion, for more than 40 years.

CONTENTS

INTRODUCTION

This book is the second edition of Customize Wall Street.

I would like readers to be aware of some important themes and messages I've woven throughout the book. I hope you will keep an eye out for them, as I feel they can enhance your understanding of my approach to reducing stress and worry when dealing with Wall Street investments.

The sequence in which these various themes appear is not indicative of their importance. I hope each of them, as well as others presented in the book, will resonate with you as being relevant in taking control of your financial future.

The first theme I want to mention deals with identifying and understanding things you can control versus that which you cannot control. Extensive financial information is dispensed in the media, so much so that it can drive us crazy. Most of it we cannot control or deal with directly. Most of us cannot control or impact solutions that are necessary. On the other hand, there are enough issues in our financial lives over which we can exercise control.

I urge you to treat with far greater importance those things over which you can exercise control, and to avoid losing sleep over issues about which you can do nothing to change. Although it makes perfect sense to be aware of what's going on in the world around us, but if you can't do anything about such things, I suggest you leave it at that. You and I cannot control changes in interest rates, inflation, the price of gasoline, the cost of real estate, or the ups and downs of stock prices.

On the other hand, if someone loses a job, that's personal, and should be dealt with directly. It is certainly within a person's control to decide whether or not to seek alternative employment. Improve your frame of mind by understanding that which you can control, and that which you cannot.

Another important theme or message you should be aware of relates to combining the actions of both saving and investing. Most of us are conditioned to think of saving and investing as two separate processes. Throughout these pages, I strongly suggest people seeking to build a nest that for greater success toward reaching whatever goals you set, that you treat saving and investing as one integrated process. I contend that the combination of both actions will greatly enhance your probability of attaining your financial goals.

Most of us grew up learning lessons on how to save. Perhaps we dropped loose change into a piggy bank. Later in life, with the reality of gaining employment, and maybe raising a family, we were exposed to the potential of making financial investments. Along with that, many of us wondered if we had sufficient monetary resources with which to buy stocks, bonds, mutual funds, annuities, or maybe even rental real estate.

As examples in the book will show, the combined discipline of saving and investment, combined as a continuous process, can yield better success than either of those disciplines alone.

One example of this combined saving and investing process is the well-known employee retirement program, usually referred to as 401(k) qualified retirement plans. These plans are authorized under the US Internal Revenue Code. Employees participating in a 401(k) plan each select a dollar amount that is taken out of each and every pay check. That amount is the savings portion, that is then regularly invested in a mutual fund which the employee has chosen. That is the investment portion of the process. Years later, at the time of retirement, employees are often surprised that the size of their retirement nest egg is larger than it might have been had they merely saved, without investing the funds in question.

Many employees who stick to the 401(k) savings and investing plan for the duration of their careers, look back and realize the discipline of saving a small portion of every pay check was not as painful as they first thought it might be. The reward of growing a nice size retirement nest egg was well worth the effort.

One more important theme that I hope you will pay attention to, involves an important question I raise early in the book. In the first section, I highlight a key question that each of us should ask of ourselves. Are you an investor or a speculator? Many folks probably answer one way, that they are investors, but soon learn that they are really the opposite.

My premise in this book is that most of us would be much better off, in our attempts to attain our financial goals, if we learn to act and think like investors, rather than speculators. Unfortunately, that is often easier said than done. In the section of the book where I address the challenges of Wall Street, we learn that many of the messages pronounced by Wall Street, and by the financial media, make that very difficult for us to do.

For reasons I explain in the book, if you approach the ownership of stocks and other investments solely for the purpose of seeing the price go up, I contend that you are more of a speculator, rather than an investor. Your approach is similar to a person who goes to a casino and I don't see how that is any different from going to a casino hoping to pick a correct number or the right color at the roulette wheel. And, when you're wrong, you lose your entire bet.

On the other hand, if a primary purpose behind buying a certain stock is to collect its dividends, which is the cash flow it regularly pays to its shareholders, then I feel you are acting as an investor. In addition, if the price of the stock goes down in the future, you haven't lost your entire investment. And, if you are making continuous investments and purchase more of the same stock at a reduced price, the dividends you receive potentially increase the percentage rate of return you receive from owning the stock in question. This pattern is more consistent with that of an investor, and not a speculator.

There are numerous other common messages and themes in this book. The ones just mentioned are but a few of the more important ones.

Customize Wall Street is divided into four sections:

1) The Challenges of Wall Street

2) Ten Powerful Tools of Investing

3) Your Financial Plan

4) Putting It All Together.

Section 1 starts with a simplified overview of Wall Street. I present a brief introduction to the stock market, Wall Street investment firms, and the financial media that deals with the world of finance.

This section presents a variety of challenges, or what I also call Wall Street "distractions". Many of these distractions are actually true and accurate, and not false in any way. But, I present them not as falsities, but as distractions from their endeavors of attaining their primary financial goals.

The list in this section of 30 distractions or challenges is not exhaustive of all sources of worry and stress one can encounter dealing with Wall Street. I feel that the list includes a sufficient variety of them to illustrate one of the major purpose I wrote this book. I truly feel that everyone who desires to take control of their financial future, should be able to do so with reduces stress and worry.

The remaining sections present approaches to setting goals and implementing plans for potential successful attainment of them, with less stress and worry than often accompanies such endeavors.

Section 2 presents Ten Powerful Tools of Investing. Many of these tools were evolved from pure common sense, such as the power of compounding, and the power of treating stock investing similar to that of running a small business. Other tools were derived from approaches I have developed in my capacity as a mutual fund portfolio manager.

These tools are consistent with my approach to value investing, which has certain attributes different from those of other portfolio managers. I feel that virtually all stock investors, whether they be professionals or private individuals, are encouraged to pick and choose from among them, that best suit their respective investment styles.

Development of these powerful tools was influenced by my readings about well-regarded portfolio managers, such as Warren Buffett, Peter Lynch, Benjamin Graham, Charles Munger, Michael O'Higgins, and Geraldine Weiss.

This section will consist of an overview, including examples, related to each of the powerful tools. Depending on the category of financial investments one chooses, all the tools, or just some of them, will apply.

The tools presented in this book are not necessarily the only ones available, to be successful at saving and investing. There are definitely others that one might use. These ten are the ones that I feel are the most powerful for my purposes when managing portfolios from a value perspective.

In a future book, I will present further expansion and explanation of not only these ten tools, but on some additional ones as well.

Section 3 presents Your Financial Plan. It gets into the "meat and potatoes" of how this book can be an essential guide, with or without the help of a financial professional, to save and invest toward a secure financial future.

In this section I introduce and explain Five Core Questions anyone can ask and answer related to one's own personal situation, related to building a nest egg for attaining financial goals. Answers to these questions will provide an easy to understand plan, that when implemented will assist in attaining whatever financial goal a person or family seeks to achieve.

In my view, you don't have to be a perfectionist while implementing whatever financial plan you've created. Partial success in the building of your desired nest egg, is still success. Going through the process of saving and investing over a long period of time, clearly shows that you're ahead of where you'd be if you had done nothing.

This section of the book concludes with some realistic illustrations. Those related to building up a retirement nest egg, include illustrating the years when a retiree starts spending down portions of the nest egg during the remainder of one's life expectancy.

Section 4, is called Putting It All Together. It covers various types of accounts savers and investors can use to safely hold their assets. These can be bank accounts, brokerage accounts, or advisory accounts under contracts with reputable financial firms. Access to reputable firms is available both online and in person, depending on one's comfort level.

In addition, I present a brief summary of the more common investment categories that people might be familiar with, and might desire to access. Whether it be real estate, stocks, mutual funds, small businesses, or collectibles, people have choices regarding methods and categories for building their financial nest eggs. The principles and approaches in this book can apply to any of them.

I also use this section to present a couple final illustrations, focusing on using most, if not all, of the ten powerful tools for saving and investing. These final examples introduce slightly more enhanced stock investment knowledge, so reading through them more than once might be essential for one to fully understand their effectiveness. I did my best to explain these examples in a way that even novice investors will get value out of reading them.

In conclusion, I hope this book accomplishes my primary goal of allowing anybody who so wishes to take advantage of the powerful tools for saving and investing that Wall Street has to offer, and that they do so with reduced stress and worry.

Each of us should be able to take control of our own financial future, and be able to sleep soundly at night, through the entire process. Recognizing and understanding what you cannot control, and what you can control, should go a long way toward helping us all in our attempt to achieve our financial dreams.

SECTION 1:

THE CHALLENGES OF WALL STREET

WHAT'S WALL STREET ALL ABOUT?

The New York Stock Exchange is located on the corner of Wall Street and Broad Street in the financial district of lower Manhattan. Just a few blocks away on Trinity Place is the American Stock Exchange. Along with the NASDAQ, the primary electronic stock exchange, these entities are often considered the center of what most stock investors refer to as Wall Street. In fact, today almost all stock trading is computerized, and the retention of formal stock exchanges serves as a primarily nostalgic value rather than as a necessity for the trading of stocks in both large volumes and small. When referring to Wall Street as an entity, it also includes all the major wire house brokerage firms and investment banking firms. Simply stated, for purposes of this book, references to Wall Street are merely a shortcut for referring to investments in the stock market.

To the extent it stands for New York finance and the broader world of stock market investing, Wall Street has a rich history.

Its history is integral to the history of American economy and finance. Our economy is often measured by landmark events in our stock market. The market crashes of 1929 and 1987 are often referred to as key turning points in our economic development. The stock market is often used as a forecasting tool, or leading indicator, for the economy in general. It has historically made moves, sometimes favorable and sometimes unfavorable, before other economic indicators. The longest running bull market in our history, covering much of the 1980s and all of the 1990s, began in August 1982, at a time when no one expected it. In contrast, the first decade of the new century marked the severest downturn in our economy since the Great Depression of the 1930s, first with a bursting of the dot-com bubble in 2001, and later the failure of subprime mortgage financing in 2008 and 2009. The combined effect witnessed a relinquishing of much of the stock market gains of the bull market of the 1980s and 1990s.

With all that said, Wall Street and the general stock market continue to provide ample opportunities for individuals and institutions to accumulate tremendous wealth. In my opinion, these opportunities mean that Wall Street has far greater importance than merely serving as a reflection of key turning points in our economy. Wall Street offers the most awesome and accessible tools for investing that will allow anyone using them to their advantage to potentially meet their most important financial aspirations. As you will see during the course of this book, the element of time is a critical key to successful investing. In most situations, it often takes longer to achieve your goals than desired. But, everyone who makes a concerted effort to save and invest has the potential for success—allowing enough time for your plan to work. The problem is that Wall Street, and the media reporting on the markets, and other economic activities, distorts the impact of financial and economic events. The messages are frequently delivered in such an alarmist fashion that they distract us from what is important in our saving and investing programs, causing us to make improper or unnecessary shifts. As we will discuss in later sections: we need to let time do its work; we need to let compounding do its work; we need to let dollar cost averaging do its work. It takes patience, discipline, and consistency to attain your financial goals, which applies to most of life's endeavors. But, in exchange, the prize is well worth it.

The purpose of this section of the book is to introduce a substantial cross section of Wall Street messages and expressions, often repeated and even exaggerated by the financial media that, more often than not, distracts and misleads the average American. The effect of these distractions often results in dissuading individuals on a large scale from carrying out their common sense, rational, and straightforward saving and investing programs.

Just as important, methods used by Wall Street firms to market themselves, and to convey their messages, have the effect of dramatically increasing stress levels and reducing comfort levels and confidence in a substantial majority of the investing public. Investors become programmed to fear down markets, and worse, they are induced to think they need to predict the direction of the market to become successful investors.

I firmly believe that my experience has taught me that the discipline of consistent, systematic saving and investing need not be a stressful endeavor, and that predicting the moves of the market or the economy is not a requirement for successfully building a financial nest egg. The two are mutually exclusive. Wall Street's ever-present message that investors need to time the market, and rotate from sector to sector, is at the very least distracting, and at its extreme, a major contributor to the stress and fear of most Americans seeking to build personal nest eggs through the use of the powerful tools the stock and bond markets have to offer. I sincerely believe that irrespective of stock prices and interest rates rising and falling, a systematic, disciplined, patient investing plan can be implemented and be largely stress-free and profitable. I believe that the tortoise and the hare parable applies to long-term, steady investing. There may be times of economic slowdown, but the media and Wall Street does not do us a favor by making us think all is lost, and there will never again be good times. History has shown time and again that patience and discipline will allow all of us in this free market capitalistic economy to build a financial nest egg, during all economic conditions.

In this section of the book, I will begin by presenting the distractions and misleading messages that Wall Street promotes, markets, or disseminates to the investing public. In many cases, these messages appear to be truthful or even axiomatic, from the perspective of traditional investors. But, when we dig deeper, we find that there is often an underlying agenda that misleads us, confuses us, or distracts us from our true investment endeavors. When we analyze them at their core, we will see that they are attempts to program us into pulling the trigger and engage in trading, either buying or selling, sooner and more frequently than we otherwise would do. Though other authors have presented "myths of Wall Street," this book will refer to them as "misconceptions" because they are not myths; they are real, and they proactively distract, confuse, and mislead us.

The list of misconceptions is by no means exhaustive or universally agreed upon by all who are critical of Wall Street. My list is presented with a twofold purpose. Firstly, I want readers to start to see a pattern in the types of misconceptions and confusing messages Wall Street disseminates, so that you can understand the motivation behind disseminating the misconceptions. Secondly, knowing that the list is not exhaustive, if you are a saver and investor you will almost definitely be confronted with other hard-sell messages. Thus, I want to empower you with an understanding and fortitude to resist being distracted and deterred from your agenda.

As a final note before delving into this section of the book, of the numerous ideas and themes I will present in these pages, there are two that readers should keep in mind throughout all sections and topics presented in these pages. Firstly, I feel it is important for the reader to frequently think about, and eventually decide, is he or she is an "investor" or a "speculator." This issue will be addressed shortly and referred to frequently throughout the book. Secondly, I will encourage readers to constantly divide variables, events, and phenomena they encounter in the world of finance and economics, into two categories—those things you can control, and those things you cannot control. We cannot control if the markets go up and down. If you decide to set aside fifty dollars per paycheck to invest in your employer's 401(k) plan, you can control that. You will be encouraged within these pages to spend more time and energy on that which you can control, and not on those elements over which you have no control.

Discipline, consistency, and patience are critical ingredients of a successful recipe for saving and investing toward reaching your financial goals and dreams. Even though there are no guarantees in the world of finance and economics, avoidance of distractions and sticking to your plan are actions each of us can control, at least to a substantial degree. Let's put our energies into things we can control, and this should take us a long way toward reducing stress and increasing the probability of success.

WALL STREET'S DISTRACTIONS

The point of this section is not to bash Wall Street or to discourage you from participating in the world's finest group of financial institutions. The goal in this section is to help make you aware of the broad spectrum of distractions and obstacles in achieving your financial goals, which emanate from Wall Street's approach to marketing its products and services. There are a certain number of Wall Street sayings, or a certain amount of common Wall Street dialogue that unfortunately perpetuate misconceptions—or as I call them, distractions—preventing Wall Street professionals, along with a vast number of their clients and customers, from successfully and efficiently achieving their financial goals and peace of mind. These distractions are presented and perpetuated by both Wall Street and a majority of investors, but once you are aware of them, you can be better suited to ask the right questions, make the right decisions, and take the right steps implementing a well-devised plan to achieve your financial goals.

Writers and commentators have frequently addressed the "myths" of Wall Street. These often consider misconceptions promulgated by the public relations and marketing divisions of the big Wall Street investment firms. These bullet phrases or common cocktail party expressions are also distractions. They get all of us wrapped up in showing how clever we are in dealing with the stock market and the numerous alternative investment programs presented by Wall Street to the investing public. In reality, virtually all of these expressions and sound bites carry a small kernel of truth, but, in the big picture, they tend to throw all of us off the path to successful saving and investing toward the achieving of our financial goals. In the following pages, I will present a cross section of well-known phrases and expressions that—if followed and adhered to—will distract us from the efficient pursuit of financial success, without the stress and worry that most of us endure.

One last point about the names or titles of each of the distractions listed below. Some of them are catchphrases or expressions often stated by either the media or Wall Street professionals or even members of the investing public. Those will be stated in quotes. Other distractions represent Wall Street processes, investment styles or categories, and axiomatic truths believed and followed by the entire industry. The reason I bring them up is that even though they are truths that I subscribe to, they still represent distractions from the real work of saving and investing efficiently and wisely in the attempt to meet our individual financial goals.

Distraction #1: "Are You an Investor or a Speculator?"

As customers and clients of Wall Street, almost all of us would say we are investors, not speculators. But are we correct in our self-assessment? This misconception alone underscores the central theme and purpose of this book.

An investor is defined as a saver, depositor, financier, shareholder, or one who backs an enterprise seeking to share in its earnings and profits. A speculator is defined as a gambler, risk taker, venture taker, deal maker, trader, or one who puts capital into an opportunity with higher than average risk, seeking higher than average return. One who engages in quick trades, or buys a stock, an option, or a commodity for quick gains, would seem to be a speculator. One who purchases stocks or bonds to earn dividends or interest payments, and intends to hold them for the long term, would be categorized as an investor.

Anyone who purchases a stock or other instrument for the primary purpose of selling that instrument at a higher price *is* a speculator, a trader, and *is not* an investor. If a person buys a piece of land, not with the intent of developing it or cultivating it, but to hang on to it until it increases in value, that person is a land speculator. The same is true for buying stocks. Most people, including the media and Wall Street professionals, talk about stocks from the perspective of how much they made from the price increase. We all do it. I have to admit that we are all speculators, to a degree. Wall Street encourages speculation by encouraging rapid buying and selling, rather than long-term saving and investing. The important distinction we need to make, as it relates to implementing a plan for your financial future, is that investing is for the long term, and can be done with a highly reduced amount of stress and worry. Engaging in speculation is fast paced and stressful.

Distraction #2: "Did Your Stock Portfolio Beat the Index?"

Where to begin on this one? The success or failure of most mutual fund managers and of investment advisors handling their clients' investments is usually measured by comparing their performance to that of a benchmark index. A benchmark really means a standard by which success or failure is measured. In most cases, the standard benchmark for measuring success in the stock market is either the S&P 500 Index or the Dow Jones Industrial Average.

People often ask whether a portfolio manager beat S&P 500 or the Dow Jones during the last twelve-month period. As a result, many advisors lose clients when the answer is no, and they will attract new clients when the answer is yes. More importantly, individuals themselves will feel like failures if their investments do not beat the Dow Jones or the S&P 500. But this measurement of success is flawed in numerous ways.

Both Wall Street and the investing public buy into this measure of investment success. If that's the case, why is the idea of beating a benchmark index viewed as a misconception? Benchmark indices are concepts that almost all investors can relate to and understand.

Let's think about this. The nature of this book is about investing with purpose and focus. It is axiomatic that the purpose of any investment program is to achieve a financial goal. If an investor feels that the purpose of investing is to "keep score," the only scoreboard an investor need is one measured in dollar signs. We cannot take "benchmark" results to the bank. Let me illustrate the point.

A few years back, a friend and I were talking about investment success. These were during times when the markets were strong, and most people were experiencing positive investment returns, and in many cases, double-digit annualized increases in their investment portfolios. At one point in our discussion, I asked him how he measured his portfolio success. I was expecting him to brag about 20% or 25% returns, or whatever was common cocktail party talk of the day. He surprised me. He told me that he didn't really understand all the sophisticated numbers, and he didn't really care how well or poorly anybody else was doing with their investments. He told me his measure of success was quite simple. At the end of each month, he looked at his brokerage statement. If the total value in his account was greater than it was in the previous month, he felt great. If the dollar amount was less than the month before, he felt bad. As long as "the money in the bank" was growing, he knew he was progressing toward his financial goals. Enough said.

The reason the idea of beating benchmarks and beating standardized indices is a misconception is that even if you beat the index, that's not necessarily money in the bank—it doesn't necessarily mean that you made money. Beating the index simply means you can brag to friends at a cocktail party that you are above average. But you can't pay your mortgage, or send the kids to college, or set a date for retirement with the claim that you beat the S&P 500 Index last year. Sure, if for example, the Dow Industrials was down last quarter by 15% and your portfolio was down only 5%, you may be smarter or luckier than the rest of the population. But let's face it: you still lost money. We all probably lost money.

Wall Street is certainly entitled to have measuring sticks so we can assess portfolio managers who are better than average, or below average, or just average. But that information only goes so far. If, for instance, performance ratings are measured on a calendar-year basis, and most investors do not put money into the stock market precisely on December 31 or January 1, they are not going to experience rates of return equal to the data published about professional portfolio managers. The public often misunderstands this and relies too heavily on information that does not apply to them. We all feel good bragging that we beat the S&P 500 or whatever index we are using. But isn't it all about building a nest egg? Shouldn't we be bragging (at least internally) that we grew our bank accounts by so many dollars? As long as we are on target to meet our financial goals, it makes no difference whether or not we are ahead of somebody else's measuring stick.

Standardized indices and benchmarks serve a valuable purpose. But to place them on a pedestal as the be-all and end-all of investment success is indeed a misconception on both the part of Wall Street and by the investing public. The true measure of the success of any investor is whether or not the investor increased the value of his or her investment portfolio during any stated length of time. More specifically, the question is whether or not the investor is on track in progressing toward his or her investment goals. Everything else is window dressing, bragging rights, and a misconception by all concerned.

Distraction #3: "How Will the Stock Market Do Tomorrow / Next Month / Next Year?"

Many of us drive ourselves crazy asking *what will the stock market, or any particular stock, do tomorrow, next week, next year?* Most of us do not do that with the value of our homes, or our life insurance policies, or even the value of the company or entity we work for. So why do we do this with our Wall Street investments?

This distraction is a true misconception perpetuated by Wall Street professionals and ourselves as members of the investing public. The truth is, nobody knows the future. For many years, Wall Street insiders have perpetuated a mystique that they have access to some special information so they can predict the direction of individual stocks or the entire stock market. Sometimes they get paid for making these predictions, and sometimes they do it with no other purpose than to show how knowledgeable they are. To add credibility to their prophecies, they offer reasons for the direction and dollar amount of their visions. One entertaining reason often given for the market going up is that "there are more buyers than sellers," or the reverse if the market is going down. I think a more sellable explanation derives from the axiomatic economic principle that "the demand exceeded the supply" in the case of rising prices, and the reverse if prices are going down.

We, the investing public, have come to expect predictions from Wall Street gurus, and we often act as if we rely on them. It is my observation that anybody, even little old ladies who form an investment club, can get lucky when guessing the direction and dollar amount of changes in stock prices. In reality, there is no crystal ball—at least not for those of us who follow the rules against illegal tactics such as insider information or attempts to manipulate the market.

The financial media continually asks Wall Street professionals probing questions: How long will this bull market or bear market last? What will the market do next year? I have been interviewed many times and have been asked those very questions. And yes, I have been flattered by the opportunity to be interviewed, so even I give them my best guess.

The flaw in perpetuating this kind of question and answer give-and-take is that it implies there is some special body of knowledge that allows Wall Street regulars to be able to guess the future better than the average investor who understands the investment process. I believe that is not the case. They can no more predict stock market movements than they can consistently predict the outcome of thoroughbred racing, or who will win the World Series (at the beginning of the season). For example, back in 2009, at the bottom of the downward spiral of the stock market, just as many Wall Street insiders and financial media were predicting that the bottom was nowhere in sight, and both the professionals and the public were certain the bottom would continue to drop out. Did anybody in March 2009 predict that by early 2013, the stock market would have regained all of its losses from the top of the market in late 2007, and go on to a new high ground? A select few might answer yes. But that's the point: the financial media, the mainstream Wall Street professionals, and the general public did not.

An even more important reason why asking one another what the future looks like for stock prices is that successful use of the power of Wall Street *does not require that information.* Let's be realistic. We all want the stock market to go up. But it does not have to go up all the time for the average person to be successful in his or her saving and investing toward their financial goals. We already know that the stock market, and the economy in general, do both. It goes up and down. We just don't usually know when. So what? If we are savers and investors for the long term, we'll get both types of moves. Since the long-term bias of the market is up, mainly because there is that one item called inflation, if our savings and investing programs are for the long term, then our rationally selected investments are going to go up. We don't need to predict the date or the target prices.

Techniques for long-term saving and investing—using the simple, but powerful tools that Wall Street provides—will be provided in the later sections of the book.

A final comment on wanting to know the future direction and dollar amount of changes in stock prices: If, in fact, someone could accurately predict stock price movements, they would not only be filthy rich, but they would be smart to keep those predictions to themselves. If you could accurately predict the outcome of a horse race and if you publicized it to the world, everyone would make a bet on the predicted winner, and no one would make any serious money. If someone could predict the winning numbers in a lottery, and publicized it to the world, the entire universe would share the winning number, and nobody would get rich. In reality, claiming that you know or believe the future price of anything does not make it come true.

The moral of this part of the story is to make investment decisions on other factors and not on someone's prediction of price movement of the stock market or any stock in particular. Seeking that type of information, and believing that type of information is required to be a successful saver and investor, is a misconception and indeed distracting.

Distraction #4: "Past Performance Is No Guarantee of Future Results."

This statement is regularly given by Wall Street on all of its advertising, and is usually posted as a disclaimer on all of its literature. I wholeheartedly agree that it is a true and important statement to make, and this type of warning is consistent with federal regulations that actually require it. So why is this a misconception?

The reason it is presented as a Wall Street misconception is the fact that Wall Street says this out of one side of its mouth and then disregards it out of the other side. Wall Street firms all sell their mutual funds and best portfolio managers based on their past performance. They then publish this type of warning, and treat it as if they have adequately cautioned people to be careful. If a mutual fund or a portfolio manager has had an extremely good performance for the prior year, let's say 20% or even higher, an advertisement plugging this success is not diminished by a caveat in fine print that no one can read without a magnifying glass that past performance is no guarantee of the future. Let's face it; the advertisement was placed there with the clear implication that this is the kind of performance one can expect to happen again if the investor just gives them their money. The warning is there for a reason.

The bottom line is that either past performance is important or it is not. Tell it to us straight, Wall Street. Which is it? The reason everyone who runs a fund or a portfolio management service is required to give the past performance warning is that the regulating agencies know that no one can predict future prices or future investment returns. And, if the regulators know this, so do all the Wall Street professionals.

So why is everything sold on Wall Street based on selling past performance? The answer lies in the root problem of the way Wall Street's products and services are sold and marketed. Every stock investment is sold on the basis of price changes. If you buy XYZ stock at the current price, you will be able to sell at a certain target price. And when you buy and sell a product based on its expected price change, it is speculation, or a wager, or a gamble!

Wall Street does not seem to want to sell its equity products—shares of common stock of publicly traded companies—on the basis of what owning the stock will do for you. If sold on that basis, it is an investment. If they said, "Currently, you will receive a dividend of such and such, but based on the company's history, you can expect dividend increases over time, so that your investment yield will eventually be such and such"—that is an investment. But because this ladder method generally results in far less buying and selling, Wall Street does not make as much money and is, therefore, less interested in this method. However, you should be!

Wall Street uses various models, such as the highly regarded dividend discount pricing model, as a means of setting a current value on a stock, to then be compared to its actual price in the market. This thinking tends to support the price movement theory of buying and selling securities. If Wall Street used the dividend discount model to set a target-dividend yield, this would support an investment approach to buying and selling stocks. Price speculation would be removed from the equation.

As members of the investing public, we buy into this misconception as well. We read the warning, we hear our investment professionals tell us this caveat, yet we disregard it as readily as does Wall Street advertising. How many "stars" does this or that fund have? The rating agencies award their stars based on past performance, and the investors reject the investments with only one or two stars, opting for the ones with four and five stars. We are all convinced that certainly those stocks or funds with the maximum ratings will have the best performance in the future. Past performance is no guarantee. Thanks for the warning, but we'll stick with the ones that kicked butt last quarter.

Is there a solution to this dilemma? Probably not. There is a certain amount of logic behind us concluding that an investment that has done well in the past will be better off in the future as opposed to those that have not done as well. What's the point of keeping records if this is not the case?

But there is an important message, however, in the warning against relying too heavily on past performance. The stock market can be quite fickle. Nobody has been proven to be able to predict the future both accurately and consistently. Many of us have been lucky in guessing the direction of the market or a particular investment—occasionally. Many a high-flying stock or mutual fund has, without warning, suddenly fallen out of favor. Beware! The warning says there is no "guarantee." Heed it! Prepare around it. Have exit strategies. Don't bet the farm; rather, diversify and play the probability game.

Distraction #5: "Why Did the Stock Market (or Any Stock) Go Up (or Down)?"

Wow, are we brainwashed! The stock market, or, in some cases, one of our stocks, goes up or down and everybody feels they have to know the reason why. The Wall Street pundits want to know why, the media wants to know why, the economists need to know why, and certainly the investing public is convinced that it's important for them to know why. The truth of the matter is, it doesn't matter why. Your stock either went up or it went down. You can deal with it as you see fit, but the reason for the move can't change whether you made money, or lost money.

I'm wondering what the more radical statement is for me to make: will I shake up more people if I say, "Hey look, the emperor is naked; he's not wearing any clothes!" Or, will I suffer banishment forever if I exclaim to the world the following: "Searching for the reason that the stock market, or any single stock for that matter, goes up or down has no practical value whatsoever!" The reason I make such a bold statement is that it occurs to me that there is little to no value to knowing the answer, even if we were able to get a correct one.

To put this whole issue to rest, let me offer the only true reason stocks go up or down. This answer is documented by every trading desk at every brokerage firm in the industry. If, during any period of time, more shares of a stock are purchased than are sold, the price of the stock will generally rise. On the other hand, if, during any time frame, more shares are sold than are purchased, the price of the stock will generally decline. This phenomenon is a direct product of the principle of supply and demand. When more people buy than sell, prices increase. When more people sell than buy, prices decline. Any other reasons given for stock prices rising or falling are unimportant, and have little or no value in helping a person make investment decisions. It is the fact of prices going up or down that is important, not the reason for such price movements. The only important questions you should be asking are: what does this mean for my overall financial plan and are there any adjustments I need to make?

Distraction #6: "What's the Best Way to Make Money in Stocks? Buy Low, Sell High."

The legendary investor of the 1930s Depression years, Bernard Baruch, is credited as giving us this oft-quoted statement in response to the following probing question: "What has been your secret to success in the stock market?" His common-sense response was, "Buy low, sell high." Since that time, this phrase has forever been regarded as words of wisdom, often mentioned alongside other glib statements, such as, "You can never go broke taking a profit" and "Do you have any good tips?" How can there be anything misleading with these expressions? These seem perfectly logical and good advice on the surface. But, upon more careful examination, the concept of buy low, sell high can play right into positioning you as a gambler— rather than an investor—and misdirect you toward Wall Street's weaknesses rather than its strengths.

The subliminal message underscoring the phrase "buy low, sell high" is the suggestion that to be a successful stock investor, one must be continually buying and selling stocks. Wall Street makes its money on the commissions earned from large volumes of stock trading. If one considers the huge number of shares traded every day on the New York Stock Exchange and the NASDAQ exchange, often exceeding a billion shares, the dollar volume is tremendous. So, of course, stockbrokers and professional traders are more concerned about the trading volumes than they are about whether the investing public has made or lost money. Wall Street's professionals want to promote a high volume of trading, so they send the politically and ethically correct sounding message, "buy low, sell high." What some astute investors feel they are really saying is: "Buy and sell, early and often."

One philosophy I have followed during the years I have managed portfolios professionally is if I find a company whose financial statements I like, and if I had the billions it would take to buy the whole company (which I don't), I will willingly buy the number of shares in that company that I can afford. Once I buy those shares, as long as the company stays strong, its price movement will take care of itself. My job is to continually monitor the financial strength of the company, and the price movement will take care of itself.

In summary, the reason "buy low, sell high" is one of Wall Street's misconceptions is because it sends a message that investors need to do constant trading in the markets. The true expression should be: "Buy at a good price and don't sell unless you need to." If you are an investor, then invest, because investing implies buying and holding on for the long term.

Distraction #7: The Stock Market is Only Good When It Goes Up

Whenever newscasters report on the stock market, they are always jovial and upbeat when the market is up, and pessimistic and depressed when the market is down. Yet, when reports on so many other segments of the economy indicate lower numbers—such as inflation, interest rates, unemployment, gasoline, and food prices—they are viewed as good reports that are good for the stock market. So why are we programmed by Wall Street and the media to feel depressed when the prices of stocks are down, and why is this a misconception?

The answer is similar to many of the misconceptions. Because of the commission structure and the importance of volume trading over quality trading for Wall Street, we are programmed to think that we should sell our stocks or make drastic changes the moment the stock market is down. Similarly, we are programmed to feel that we should sell whenever the market goes up. Collectively, we are all at fault for thinking this way.

In business, does every entrepreneur feel that when inventory costs rise that business comes to a screeching halt and no one is going to buy their products anymore? If inventory or raw materials costs rise or fall, or utility costs or rents increase, the business entity merely adjusts their selling prices to reflect their desired profit margins. In real estate, as market prices rise, property owners note the increasing equity values, but it doesn't suddenly drive them to put their properties up for sale. When real estate values decline, many investors who have available cash or access to financing start searching for properties to purchase at lower valuations, knowing that rental incomes will result in higher returns. When gasoline prices fall, or one's favorite department store has a sale at the end of the fashion season, the lines are out the door to take advantage of the bargains. Why isn't this true with stocks? It should be. Whether up or down, there is a positive opportunity.

As with many of the misconceptions, both Wall Street and the investing public share responsibility for their response to stock market price fluctuations. In reality, stock market downturns offer investors the opportunity to add to their portfolios at discounted prices. Later, when the market improves, and stock prices turn upward, these same investors will reap greater profits, because their "inventory" was purchased at lower prices. The reality is that stock prices go up and down. Each condition provides opportunities for investors, and one should not be favored over the others. More importantly, neither condition, up market or down market, should cause fear, stress, or concern.

In conclusion, the reason that giving investors the impression that the only good market is an up market is misleading, and outright wrong, is that people who take that view miss some wonderful opportunities to purchase stocks at a discount, and to eventually enjoy excess profits. In fact, some investors feel it is far safer to invest during market downturns because the market has shaken out some of the potential risks involved in stock investing.

Distraction #8: Technical Analysis Versus Fundamental Analysis

When investors are asked whether they use technical analysis or fundamental analysis regarding their stock selection process, the misconception is inherent to the question itself.

Both fundamental analysis and technical analysis are well-accepted methods used for stock research and for deciding which stocks to place in your portfolio. The misconception lies in the asking of whether an investor uses one method or another—suggesting that one is better than the other. Why are they viewed as being mutually exclusive? There is no reason that both techniques cannot be employed for isolating favorable stocks in which to invest.

There is more to this misconception. It lies in the fact that one of the techniques is a valid research tool for promoting sound investing, while the other is a highly developed and highly recognized tool attempting to increase the probability of being successful in stock speculation. Fundamental analysis is the study of financial statements of publicly traded entities, prepared by CPAs and auditing firms. Technical analysis is the study of charts of historical price movements of stocks, options, and commodities. To the extent both techniques provide investors and speculators with a sense that they can increase the probability of predicting the future about stocks, technical analysis attempts to predict the future movement of stock prices, whereas fundamental analysis attempts to predict the future about the economic soundness of the underlying companies. There is some overlap between the two analytical techniques, which involves looking at well-accepted economic ratios, such as price-to-book ratio, price-to-earnings ratio, and price-to-sales ratio, all on a per share basis.

So in what way does Wall Street promote a misconception by recognizing and supporting those analysts who use either or both methods? As implied earlier, this is one misconception that is subtle. I certainly don't purport that Wall Street professionals favor one technique over the other, because that is not the misleading part. It is more the fact that Wall Street appears to give equal credence to both techniques. One technique, fundamental analysis, is basic to the study of investments from an economic viability perspective. The other technique, technical analysis, ignores the viability of the stock or other financial instruments, and basically charts price movements. Continuously novel analytical tools are developed, aided by the continuous improvement of computer technology over the last quarter century. Each new technical system claims to have greater and more accurate predictive powers. This is speculation in its most obvious and perverse form. It has no place being given the credence and status of fundamental economic analysis.

Distraction #9: "Which Perform Better, Growth Stocks or Value Stocks?"

Everyone wants his or her stocks to grow in price. Everyone wants to buy his or her stocks at a good value price. In the minds of most stock investors, buying growth stocks means that they are buying at a premium price (high multiples), with the expectation that the company is in a growth phase and the stock will go even higher. As for value stocks, most investors feel they are buying stocks whose businesses are more mature and stable, and their only chance to make a profit is by purchasing such stocks at cheap prices. The misconception in this kind of thinking lies in the basic premise of this section that asks if you are an investor or a speculator. If your only motive and purpose in buying stocks is to follow their price movements, this suggests that you are a speculator. Investors, however, will look to the fundamental soundness of stocks they buy, and the pattern of dividend growth.

What I am pointing out with this misconception is a variation of the question: Are you a speculator, and therefore seeking price growth; or are you an investor and seeking good long-term values?

Value investors tend to use fundamental analysis while looking for stocks that appear to be priced fairly and appear to be fundamentally sound in comparison to other stocks selling for the same price. Growth investors tend to ignore the fundamentals and use technical analysis, looking for stocks possessing technical indicators that suggest potentially rapid upward swings in price.

The primary misconception promulgated by Wall Street, and accepted by its clients and customers, is that value stocks mean bargain-basement stocks. This is misleading. Let's assume for this discussion that all investors have at least a modicum of speculation in their approach to stock selections. I think all of us want our stocks to go up in price, either in the short run or the long run. As an investor, I wholeheartedly admit I share that view. However, I wish to assure you that I also consider myself to be a value investor. The most common view of a value stock is one that appears to be available at a bargain price.

What is not made clear to the general public is that a bargain price, a true value price, does not necessarily mean a cheap price. A stock can be a bargain price at $200 per share, and a stock can be extremely overpriced at $.50 a share. If all stocks priced under $1.00 per share were value stocks, why do most people who speculate in "penny" stocks lose more than they profit?

A value stock is one where the underlying financial statements of the company are fundamentally sound, and the price of the stock is such that an investor can earn a fair return over time through a combination of dividend distributions and steady increases in the stock price. Many value stocks priced over $100 per share have grown steadily to higher prices at the same rate as "bargain" priced stocks.

What many people fail to realize that if you want an investment to grow by a certain percentage (10%, 12%, or whatever), it's the number of dollars that you invest that is the important variable, not the number of shares you buy. If you have $1,000 to invest, it makes no difference if you buy 100 shares of a $10 stock or 10 shares of a $100 stock (ignoring commission costs for purposes of this illustration). In either case, if the investment goes up by 10%, the value of the investment becomes $1,100. The important variable is whether the investment is a good value or not.

What is the misconception regarding growth stocks? It is because there is an implied promise or inference that such stocks will eventually grow in value. That may or may not ever occur. If someone says they buy value stocks, people think that the investor is buying stocks at a cheap price. If the person says they wish to invest in growth stocks, there is the expectation that the stocks in question are going to automatically grow in value. Why else would they be called "growth" stocks? Realistically, value stocks have just as much potential for growing in value as do growth stocks.

Wall Street makes us believe that investors choose between value stocks and growth stocks. That distinction exists to this day, and is unlikely to change anytime soon. The misconception lies in the same distinction as the question, "Are you an investor or a speculator?" All stocks have the potential to increase in price. All stocks are a bargain at certain prices. If you use fundamental analysis for researching and selecting stocks in which to invest, the chances of finding good value stocks that will hopefully grow over time have a higher probability than using mere labels with which to choose your investments.

Distraction #10: Undervalued Stocks / Overvalued Stocks

This misconception is a euphemistic way of saying "cheap" stocks and "expensive" stocks. As used by brokers and professional advisers, there is more to the concept of overvalued and undervalued. The basic idea of overvalued and undervalued is derived from the technical analysis approach to stock research and stock selection.

Technical analysis mostly consists of zigzagging chart patterns of stock prices that slant upward when stocks prices rise, and those that slant downward when they decrease. At some point on any chart of stock prices, the upward slanting prices stop going up, and these points are called "resistance." Likewise, at some point on a chart, the downward slanting prices stop going down, and these points are called "support." If on a stock chart, the stock price rises above that "resistance" point, or the stock price declines below that "support" point, many analysts will refer to the stock as either expensive (overvalued when stock prices rise above resistance levels) or cheap (undervalued when stock prices drop below support levels), respectively.

The reason that these concepts are misconceptions from Wall Street is because of the propensity for commission-oriented broker representatives to encourage frequent trading and portfolio repositioning. The traditional Wall Street brokerage firms earn revenue and compensate their account representatives by means of trading commissions. Like real estate, when transactions occur, charging clients transaction commissions compensates the professionals arranging the trades. It does not matter if the client makes a profit or suffers a loss on the transaction; the commissions are paid.

There are indeed ethical constraints adhered to by Wall Street professionals. There must be a sound economic reason for suggesting or encouraging a stock transaction. However, Wall Street knows that clients are motivated to sell stocks at a profit. But what about the idea of buying more of the same stock if the price drops to decrease the average purchase price of your stock? Or what about staying the course because the company is sound and fluctuations are normal? These are the types of things that must be taken into account. You have a responsibility to do your own thinking when commissions are simply based on action and not the value of the action being taken.

Distraction #11: Setting a Target Price at Which to Sell a Stock

This seems reasonable and certainly begs the question, "How is this a misconception?" It is natural to set a target-selling price on anything you buy, with the intent to later resell it. Ah, but therein lies the issue. Setting a target price on what you buy with the intent to resell. When was the last time the average person bought a new home, or even an investment rental property, and immediately set a target price at which they plan to sell? They might think about it in the abstract, but rarely is it the major part of the game plan.

Why has Wall Street programmed us to be ready at all times to sell if your chosen stock hits a particular price? Naturally, buying and selling are at the core of what stock trading is all about. Each time there is a purchase and sale, the transaction price is recorded. Each of these trades gives us the stock price quotations. Because there are multi-thousands of stock names available, and billions of shares changing hands on a daily basis, Wall Street legitimately assumes that most investors want to lock in a profit—if they adhere to the buy low, sell high philosophy. So why not publicly proclaim a near-term target price that major firms believe various stocks they are following will rise to before stabilizing, and maybe giving back some of the gains?

Most stock investors and traders harbor uncertainty and stress when faced with fluctuations and volatility. Whether stock traders claim to be speculators or investors, most of them still claim to be risk adverse. This entire book is about risk adversity, stress reduction, and understanding what you can and cannot control. But let's look at this in a different context. Most participants in the stock market, investors and speculators alike, are averse to "leaving money on the table." This usually translates to one of the two following scenarios.

In one situation, a stock might be sold at a certain price, after achieving a respectable gain (perhaps at a price consistent with the broker's target price). Shortly after the sale, the stock price shoots up even higher. In this case, the investor would complain that the stock shouldn't have been sold so soon, because they would have enjoyed more gains by continuing to own the stock. In the second situation, a stock rises to a certain respectable gain (again the price might be consistent with the broker's target price), but the stock is not sold at that point, perhaps due to the optimism of even more price gains. Shortly thereafter, the stock drops in price, giving back some or all of the price gains. In this case, the investor would complain that the stock should have been sold at the recent high point, but failing to do so, the investor missed profiting from all or part of the price gain.

In both situations, money was "left on the table." But therein lies the entire misconception involved with analysts setting target prices. Wall Street sends another one of its messages encouraging frequent trading, and investors placate this mentality by setting a predetermined sell point.

Let's accept two core principles: no one, absolutely no one, can consistently predict market prices over an extended period of time, and no one can perfectly time the purchase and sale of all stocks in one's portfolio for optimum profits. We can almost always view the process as leaving some money on the table.

If you are an investor and not a speculator, here's a simple solution to the dilemma of setting a target sale price: just don't do it. If the stocks you own pay dividends, and they have a record of continually increasing their dividends, the only way you'll continue to receive the increasing dividends is to continue to own the stocks. Holding on to your stocks as long as they pay good dividends, and even show increasing dividends, means that now you're an investor, and not a gambler or speculator.

There is another reason that the idea of buying a stock and immediately setting a selling price is a Wall Street misconception. It all depends on who sets the target-selling price. If the investor sets the selling price, there may be a host of reasons for that decision by the investor. On the other hand, the broker or adviser, who might be the very person who recommended the purchase of the stock, could set the target price. The broker or advisor could justify the sale because a profit has been demonstrated, and gets the commission from taking the action where he or she would otherwise not get a commission if you did not sell.

In summary, the general policy at most Wall Street firms of setting target prices for selling stocks sends a strong message that they do not want or expect their clients and customers to hang on their investments for an extended period of time. Why not hang on if the stock is doing well and paying good dividends? This perpetuates the worry and stress investors experience when stock prices go up and down. Because stock prices and stock markets, in general, go up and down as a basic part of that industry, it is foolhardy and counterproductive for Wall Street firms to perpetuate fear and stress when an integral part of the process is to continually measure and report prices on a continuous real-time basis. I strongly believe that Wall Street firms have a responsibility to reassure their investing clients not to worry or stress when prices fluctuate and that focus should be set on the overall performance toward the investor's goals.

Distraction #12: Analysts' Opinions

The father of current stock research and analysis was Benjamin Graham, author of the 1934 text *Security Analysis*. Biographies on the life of Warren Buffett report that Graham was both an inspiration and mentor to young Buffett as he began emerging with his unparalleled portfolio management skills.

Portfolio analysis has been enhanced in recent decades with the study of modern portfolio theory, which embodies some extensive mathematical formulae designed to quantify stock valuations for investment speculation purposes. It is an extremely complex, numeric, artistic science. The highest accreditation professionals in the field can achieve is a certification as a Chartered Financial Analyst. Most supporting applications and theories are now implemented by sophisticated software programs, many of which generate institutional trading arrangements, such as "programmed trading," "risk arbitrage," "collateralized-securitized debt obligations," "interest rate swap arrangements," and many other sophisticated instruments involving currencies, commodities, and fixed income.

With all this sophistication, how can the average stock or mutual fund investor trying to figure out how to manage his or her own 401(k) plan, or set aside enough to build a college fund for the children, not be impressed with analysts' reports and recommendations? Once again, there is the subtle misconception that escapes most of us that is promoted by Wall Street and contributed to by most average investors.

To understand this misconception, it first requires understanding the audience to which this service of analysts' opinions is primarily aimed. Today, with the Internet and vast amounts of data available to everyone, most members of the public have access to the opinions of stock analysts. Public sites such as Yahoo, Google, Bloomberg, Fox Business, and Dow Jones provide a plethora of such information and data. Originally, analysts' opinions were primarily provided, for a fee, to professional and institutional portfolio managers, brokers, and advisors. Analysts' opinions tended to culminate in suggesting target prices at which stocks under review should be bought and sold. Professional advisers and account representatives were encouraged to provide such information to their clients, for to encourage the buying and selling of stocks. Sound familiar?

In summary, the purpose of offering research is a subtle way of promoting the purchase and sale stocks which the firm follows, underwrites, and in which it makes a market. In recent years, ethical rules have emerged to discourage firms from being overly aggressive in tying their research to their trading activities. So-called "firewalls" are established at firms to separate their research departments from their investment banking and from their brokerage activities.

It is not the intent or focus of this book to suggest how firms should do research, or to whom they should present their offerings. The reason I have presented this research topic as a misconception is so that you, as an investor, understand that when a Wall Street firm makes offerings of research, it is often with the intent of encouraging and justifying the action to promote or market stocks that they follow.

Distraction #13: "You'll Never Go Broke Selling a Stock for a Profit."

Where does this misconception or distraction come from? In the days when large Wall Street brokerage houses were the only means by which most Americans could buy and sell stocks, the stockbroker was king. Since the livelihood of a broker depended on generating trading commissions each month, most professionals generated commissions in two ways. They would acquire more and more clients, and they would encourage clients to make frequent trades.

To avoid the appearance of ethical impropriety, usually referred to as "churning," they felt it necessary to have economically sound reasons for suggesting their clients change existing investments. If a client made a gain from an investment, no matter how small, it could be claimed that the stockbroker was doing a good job. Clever brokers constantly came up with little sayings and catchphrases that appeared to support the economic soundness of their trading suggestions. They latched on to such phrases as "you'll never go broke taking a profit" or "buy low, sell high" or "buy on the rumor, sell on the news" and many others.

Wall Street misleads its clients and customers with this misconception by suggesting that a price increase of any kind justifies the sale of the stock. The ulterior motive simply being that Wall Street profits from the commission of trades and that any price increase affords them justification for the trade.

Of course, Wall Street professionals are not the only guilty parties in these situations. We, the clients and customers, are a bit greedy and have a limited sense of delayed gratification. We want easy riches, found money, and desire to earn a profit without a lot of work. We compromise long-term success for short-term gain. More importantly, we want to do this without exercising patience and discipline, or recognizing the amount of risk we are taking. We hear the words profit and gain, and are less dazzled by long-term strategy and slow, steady growth toward our nest eggs.

We all want our stocks to go up in price, and I certainly recognize that the client benefits when his or her stock is sold at a profit. But price increase cannot be the only consideration. Clients and brokers alike need to consider the long-term potential for a stock. Is it paying consistent dividends? Does the company have a history of growth? Will selling, because of a short-term price increase, compromise the likelihood of long-term gains? If you sold now, what would you be replacing it with to generate the same progress toward your financial goals?

A major economic concept, often heeded by academics but rarely considered by average investors, is known as "opportunity cost." The concept is simple, even if not often considered. An opportunity cost is usually defined as the gain or benefit one gives up by foregoing an investment opportunity. In a different vein, an opportunity cost is the choosing of one investment over another, and thus foregoing the greater gain one might have enjoyed if the other investment had been chosen. In reality, this opportunity cost usually occurs because one has only so much capital or funds available, and does not have enough money to invest in both investments. In the case of frequent buying and selling of stocks, the opportunity cost is that of selling stocks after holding them a short period of time, and not holding on longer to give them time fully develop and enjoy the long-term benefits, such as dividend payments and additional upside growth potential.

Successful brokers and media commentators have said for years that an investor cannot go broke taking a profit. Successful brokers and media commentators have said for years that an investor cannot go broke taking a profit. So what is the misconception for this expression? Well, let's interpret the statement as to what the broker is really saying to their client. Interpretation: Let's sell your stock now that it has moved up a couple of points so that I can earn a commission for selling it, and then I can earn another commission on the next investment we make. Is this disguised churning? We know that even though an investor certainly will not lose money if the broker sells the client's stocks at a profit, but the broker who earns commissions for every purchase and every sale of an investor's stocks will more than likely get rich, long before the client, by trading in quantity over quality.

In what other ways could this be considered a myth? If you buy a stock for $10 and sell it for $15, how could you be in danger of losing money if you keep doing that? Actually, therein lies the answer. You can indeed go broke taking a profit, if you only make a profit one time. As has been stated in prior misconceptions, the suggestion by the broker of either selling at a target price, or selling for a quick profit, implies that the broker is promoting the client as a speculator, and not a long-term investor. The broker makes a commission whenever the client buys and whenever the client sells, and it might be the underlying reason for the recommendation.

Here's the point: If a stock professional sees an opportunity for a client to earn a quick profit, and the client agrees, then the question arises, what do you invest in now? Assuming the broker recommends another stock to purchase, what makes us assume that the next stock investment will be profitable, or the one after that? Taking a profit one time cannot create an assumption that all future investments will be profitable. So the phrase suggesting that a stock investor can never go broke taking a profit assumes that every time a broker suggests a stock, the client will always be able to sell it at a profit. Selling on a recommendation that results in a profit on one occasion does not guarantee that will happen every time.

The real message here is to always question the reason for selling a stock. If the person suggesting that you sell your investment has an ulterior motive, such as generating fees for themselves, then it is urged that you should think again. If the person making the suggestion has your best interests at heart, and is not making money just because you sell, then the suggestion has much greater credibility.

Distraction #14: "Can You Recommend a Good Stock?"

We're all looking for a good stock tip. You know, the loud fellow in the fancy blazer at a cocktail party who drove up in a Bentley, and clearly knows what he's doing in the world of finance. If he would only share with us a tiny kernel of information that he has saved for us alone, we too would be booking our timeshare week at Monte Carlo or Brussels. Let's face facts. If anybody truly has a piece of special, cannot-lose information about a stock (information that no one else has), it's certainly going to be a felony violation to share that information with you. In all other cases, that individual has no greater knowledge or good common sense than you do. He or she might have been luckier over the years, you know, having been at the right place at the right time, but that cannot be relied upon as a stock tip worthy of risking your money on. The misconception here is perpetuated almost entirely by the investor that there is a quick fix to profits—if only you have the right tip.

In the management of a mutual fund, my firm uses a set of criteria to pick a basket of stocks to build a portfolio, selected from a group of companies that meet those criteria. Some of the stocks will work out better than others, and that's because we have no predictive powers. We don't have a crystal ball. What we propose is an investment style that includes a range of stocks that fall into a disciplined set of criteria. We do not make all our bets on just one stock, because that then becomes an all-or-nothing proposition.

It would be far more sensible if folks at cocktail parties asked: "What is your investment style?" People should ask about categories of stocks, or bonds, or mutual funds that other people subscribe to. Asking others about the name of one good stock is like asking for a specific color or number at the roulette table. "Hey, what do you like, number thirty-six or number twelve?" "How're you feeling about red today?" Well, if the other person is well acquainted with the magnet that can stop the ball, hidden under the tablet, and has access to the button, then that's a great question, and then you just hope you don't get caught. Otherwise, it is foolhardy at best.

It would make perfect sense to ask a seasoned stock investor if they knew the names of some stocks that pay good dividends or that have very low debt, or that have performed well during the last twelve months. If the other person is willing to share that information with you, then no harm has been done. As an investor, you would still have to decide whether the information is helpful to you. But merely asking for a good stock, or a good tip, requires judgment on the part of the person being asked the question, which he or she probably has no ability to exercise. The moral of the story is that there is no practical shortcut to sound stock investing, and asking for or receiving stock tips is nothing more than a gamble.

Distraction #15: "Can You Recommend a Good Broker or Investment Advisor?"

This misconception is mostly perpetuated by clients themselves, but sometimes by well-intentioned Wall Street professionals. In most cases, if a client recommends an advisor, broker, or portfolio manager, it is often one with good credentials and is well established at a major firm. We often get starry-eyed by John Bigbucks, or Jane Tradesalot, who is first vice president at *Hopes, Prayer & Promises*, the largest firm on the planet. It would be rare for a private individual to recommend a young man or woman just starting out in the business, eager to please the first few clients they get.

The fact of the matter is, for any broker working at a major wire house firm, the investment choices you, as a client, will receive are going to be exactly the same from the fledgling broker and from the seasoned veteran who earns $500,000 bonuses every year. Brokers themselves are not professional analysts. Their firms come out with daily and weekly recommendations for their broker staff to recommend to clients (recommendations in all investment categories). They have recommended offerings in stocks, bonds, options, and even commodities and other nonconforming investments (such as hedge funds and limited partnerships). It is not the broker's brilliance that comes up with the clever offerings. It is the broker's *brilliance* that convinces you, the client, to invest more dollars with him or her than with a competing broker down the hall. Brokers are the salesmen.

So the interpretation of this misconception is: what you need is a broker who has been successful at convincing many, many people to become clients, and has thereafter convinced many,

many clients to buy (and sell) lots and lots of stuff. What does a "good broker" mean? It all depends on your perspective or point of view. From the perspective of a potential client or investor, you would think this phrase means an investment professional who provides good service, has the client's interest at heart, and has success with his client's investments. A good broker is perceived to be a good stock picker, one who has particular insight into which stocks will do well and which stocks to avoid. They have some secret knowledge, some backroom information that allows them to separate the wheat from the chaff. For this magical ability, they are entitled to earn big dollars, and the reason their numbers of clients are large is that the reputation has spread as to their brilliance and prophetic powers. The solution to the misconception is pretty simple. The measure of a success of a stockbroker, in the eyes of the employing firm, is not how good of a return is provided to clients, but rather how many clients the broker has and how much in commissions and fees has been generated for the firm. The greater the amount of fees and commissions the broker earns, the more the broker is rewarded in base salary and bonuses. The actual performance of your investments is inconsequential in the eyes of the firm and the broker. Thus, a good broker should be one who puts your interests before theirs in the process of helping you develop your saving and investing plan.

Distraction #16: "I'll Sell as Soon as My Stock Gets Back to What I Paid for It."

This is a misconception detrimental to good portfolio management, perpetuated mostly by individual clients and investors, but often encouraged by their brokers and advisors. Investors inherently do not want to lose money. And brokers find it far easier to get investors to remain their clients if they can, at worst, break even for a client. We investors all feel it is a sign of failure if any one of our stocks loses money. We often refuse to sell it at a loss. We don't mind breaking even; we just don't want to lose. We feel that someone is testing us, and we don't want to fail. We lose sight of the fact that if a stock loses money, we didn't fail, the stock failed. The stock doesn't know the price we bought it, and its price fluctuates all over the place. So it doesn't make any sense for us to feel we have failed or are losers just because we bought at a price higher than it is today.

The lesson to be learned here relates to managing your portfolio. It is the rare investor who owns only one stock. Most people who invest own either a few stocks, or if you can afford it, many stocks. In other words, most investors own a portfolio. So whether you are a winner or a loser depends on the status of your entire portfolio, your stocks as a group. This is precisely why we diversify. Stated differently, your level of wealth with respect to your stock portfolio depends on how the group as a whole is doing. No single stock defines the well being of your entire portfolio.

Let's suppose you own five stocks in your portfolio, and four of them are doing well, and just one is doing poorly, i.e., 80% of your portfolio is strong, and 20% is weak. As long as you hold on to the one weak stock, 20% of your portfolio will remain weak. It will remain that way until your weak stock gets back to break even. But if you sell that weak stock (at a loss), now you don't have any weak stocks, assuming the other four stocks are still doing well. But if you wait in the hopes that the poorly performing stock will go back to even, then that stock will drag down the total performance of your portfolio until you get rid of it.

Had you sold the weak stock earlier, when you had decided you had one weak stock out of five, you would have been rid of the weak stock right away. Even though you would have lost money, you would have improved your cash position at the point you sold it. You would now have generated cash, which could get into a potentially good stock. Maybe you could buy more of any of the four other stocks that are doing well. If you are continuously looking for new stocks, you now have some cash to be able to buy a new stock if you find one that shows promise. The probability of making up the portion of the money you previously lost is greater with a new stock that shows potential than with the old stock that was a demonstrated loser.

Some readers might be confused by the suggestion to weed out weak stocks from your otherwise healthy portfolio. The purpose here is not to suggest frequent buying and selling, but rather to encourage discipline in managing a team of stocks. If you set a downside loss target for any stock in your portfolio, then you should adhere to that discipline, and not try to nurse any particular stock back to its "break-even" point. It's the money you want to recover, not the stock price.

As a simple example, let's assume you've decided that if any stock in your portfolio goes down more than 15% below the movements of the general stock market, then that stock has to be sold, and replaced by a stock that keeps up with the movements of the general stock market. Then we are suggesting that you stick to that discipline. In some cases, this might occur more often than not, and in other cases, such an event will occur rarely. In either event, I am trying to teach two concepts. One concept is that of discipline and consistency. The other concept is that of working with your portfolio as a team. If there is a weak member of the team, replace it with one that has stronger potential. It is the team that will keep your money on track, not any one prima donna all-star. The same concept can be applied if you have one or two stocks that are carrying your entire portfolio. Just because those two stocks are making your portfolio as a whole look good, it doesn't mean you should ignore the underperforming stocks. If a teammate is tired, they should be substituted—or the entire team will suffer.

Distraction #17: Timing the Market / Sector Rotation

Over the years, professional portfolio managers have developed a variety of trading styles and methodologies with the intent of improving investment returns and gaining a competitive advantage over other portfolio managers. Two such techniques are market timing and sector rotation. The comments and critiques about these two styles could apply equally to many other portfolio management techniques and styles.

Both market timing and sector rotation are attempts to accomplish a result that we've already discussed in a previous misconception, that of buying low and selling high. Timing the market is nothing more than developing and using signals that (hopefully) suggest to a market trader that the stock market is going to stop going in one direction.

Sector rotation is essentially the same technique, but rather than focus on the entire market or just a single security, the portfolio management invests in a basket of stocks in a certain market sector or industry that appears to have the promise of delivering higher returns than the general market. The portfolio manager develops and employs certain indicators that signal when the chosen sector will stop delivering superior returns, and hopefully signals another sector or industry that will take its place in delivering higher returns than the general market, and other sectors or industries.

There are numerous problems with this and other types of "first to the party" techniques of portfolio management. The single most obvious problem, both from the Wall Street perspective and the individual investor perspective, stems from the fact that nobody can accurately and consistently predict changes in market direction, or the price behavior of any particular stock. Simply stated, portfolio managers and individual investors who are trying to time market bottoms and tops, or rotate to better-performing industries or sectors, are just plain wrong more times than they are right.

It is true that when investments are broken down into their respective industries or sectors—such as high tech, retail, or transportation—at any one time, some of those areas are performing better than others. It is also true that the stock market often exhibits a direction or trend, usually referred to as a bullish uptrend or bearish downtrend. If a portfolio manager or individual investor can identify when the up and down trends will change direction, they will be able to maximize investment results. However, focusing on this as a sole source of investment strategy is extremely limiting and risky.

As has now been said many times, nobody can consistently pick the perfect time to change directions of their investments, or the sectors in which to make investments on a regular basis. No crystal ball is telling us in advance when these events will occur. We only learn about the changes in market trends and the better-performing sectors after the fact, on a historical basis. Over the years, there have been many clever researchers, analysts, and statisticians who have identified previously undiscovered patterns and correlating indicators that when first implemented, appeared to give them a competitive advantage in "getting to the dance early." What has historically happened is that when the style or technique becomes well known, everyone else trying to time the market or rotate sectors ends up with similar investment results, without any measurable advantage over others—when 1,000 people win the same $5,000 lottery prize. Studies have shown that when a broad spectrum of investors all chose the same time to rotate sectors, or change from buying stocks to selling stocks, nobody gets an advantage. Everybody is doing the same thing, and most everyone gets the same results—the results of the general market.

A more subtle misconception related to timing and rotating is one that hurts individual investors in a more measurable way. If investors are convinced they can gain an advantage by market timing or sector rotation, this invites a lot of active trading. Professionals who recommend this are playing the speculation game, and are not recommending their clients and customers act as long-term investors. Frequent changing of investments invites additional transaction costs, and in many cases, taxable transactions. Wall Street professionals often feel they need to recommend continual portfolio changes otherwise they may be accused of not watching the store, of not doing their job. As the client, we must take some responsibility for thinking that if our broker is not constantly making adjustments to our portfolio, they must be neglecting us.

In summary, if anyone could truly time the ups and downs of the market, or consistently rotate investments into the best-performing sectors and industries, such an individual would not need the advice of any Wall Street professional. That individual would become exceedingly wealthy without the need of anyone's help. Likewise, if any Wall Street professional could successfully time markets or rotate sectors on a consistent basis, that person would not need to ever have clients, for the same reason.

Distraction #18: Investment Diversification / Asset Allocation

Diversification of investment assets and investment categories is a basic investment philosophy, and nothing said in this book is intended to contradict that concept. It is indeed true that we should not put all our eggs in one basket. However, the valuable tool of diversification (something we will discuss in detail in the next section) and properly allocating your wealth is not necessarily offered in the most supportive manner by Wall Street.

Let's think about the metaphor for a second. It talks about not putting "eggs" in "baskets." In reality, we are placing "money" into "investments." In the real world, some baskets are stronger and easier to carry than others. Some investments turn out better than others, and are more appropriate for the kind of client involved. The purpose of the metaphor is clear. If you are walking along carrying eggs in two or three baskets, and happen to drop one of the baskets and that group of eggs breaks, there are still the remaining baskets with unharmed eggs. You haven't lost everything.

In my opinion, the value of the metaphor stops there. There are countless kinds of investments, and if you overly diversify, you could easily select so many differing investments that the good results from some investments could be negated by the poor results in some of the others. It is my impression from reading about Warren Buffett that he tried to stay away from excessive diversification, for that very reason. His portfolio held by Berkshire Hathaway is valued at so many billions of dollars that it legally *requires* him to diversify a certain amount. It is my understanding that he does not diversify for its own sake, and he avoids putting assets into any industry or company that he feels he cannot understand.

This is a great lesson related to limiting your diversification or your allocation of assets into investments you feel you can understand and that make sense based upon your individual financial goals. It is your money, and *you* have a responsibility to know not only what you are trying to accomplish (your investment goals), but also the type of investments that are best suited for accomplishing your personal goals. Putting money into a hedge fund or a commodities trading program without understanding the processes or risks is simply gambling. Remember, a theme of this book is understanding what you can control, harnessing that knowledge, and recognizing what you cannot control.

The system of asset allocation is similar to diversification, but adds an element of a market or economic timing. If you have sufficient assets to invest—over and above what you need for food, shelter, transportation, education, and other necessities of life—you must decide how to allocate the remaining dollars for future desires and needs. In addition to diversifying, in a broader sense among such categories as real property, stocks, fixed income, art and antiques, and even cash itself, asset allocation involves the percentage amounts to be placed in the various categories. For most asset allocation scenarios, the percentages are divided into stock investments, fixed income investments, real estate investments, and alternative investments. The term "alternative" merely implies other less typical investment categories, like art, antiques, or precious resources.

Asset allocation programs also include suggesting when to increase or decrease investments in the various categories you choose to invest in. The misconception here is that it now includes an element of market timing. For example, if an investor has been advised to allocate their investments as one-third in real estate, one-third in stocks, and to keep one-third in cash, these percentages might change over time. If it should happen that economic conditions change a few months later, the advisor might suggest that the investor increase the percentage in one category, and decrease it in the others.

The misconception here is that these suggested changes in allocation create problems, whether they are made in anticipation of upcoming market conditions or if they are made after conditions have already changed. If allocation changes are made after the fact, such as increasing investments in stocks because there has just been a good run-up in the market, it is like trying to jump on a train after it has left the station. Remember, past performance is no guarantee of future results. If an advisor suggests changing allocation percentages based on supposed indicators of what's coming in the economy, we then rely on our repeated statement that no one can predict future moves in the markets or the economy consistently and accurately. If they could, they would keep it to themselves, and maximize their wealth.

Investors who like the idea of a certain amount of diversification and some basic allocating of the kinds of assets in which they invest are certainly wise and reasonable. The message here is not that such comfort measures are bad, not at all. It is important that you diversify and allocate among categories with common sense based on your individual goals, knowledge, and financial position. In the next section on powerful tools, we will discuss some ideas presented to avoid the pitfalls of excessive diversification, and how to avoid attempting to time the market with your allocation of assets.

When selecting allocation percentages, the proper approach would be to analyze each category as if it were the only category to be chosen. Assuming the investor (you) has already done an analysis of long-range investment goals, the investor will already have a pretty good idea of the long-term average rate of return required to achieve those monetary goals. (Determining your long-term goals and how to identify the rate of return you will need to accomplish your goals is something I will walk you through later on.) It seems to make sense to select only those investment categories for allocation that will have the potential to deliver the long-term average rate of return desired for achieving the stated monetary goal. Why would you choose categories for investment that will underperform on average over a long period of time? It would then force the other allocation categories to have to work harder or perform better over the long haul to make up for what another category fails to deliver.

The goal of every investor is to achieve a certain amount of wealth, which will hopefully be available in the future for certain financial purposes. Owning certain investments, whether concentrated into one or two types or spread over a broad spectrum, is the owning of the tools with which to reach the goal. The goal is to acquire the money. The tools are what get you to the goal. Do not confuse the two!

It is strongly recommended that if an investor decides to diversify and allocate percentages among categories, there is no reason to continually change those percentages. The only reason to change would be if, over a sustained period of time, the category that is under performing no longer appears to have the potential to adequately achieve the average rate of return of the overall investment program.

Distraction #19: Modern Portfolio Theory / CAPM / Efficient Frontier / Dividend Discount Model

Entire volumes have been written on each of these topics. Even today, scholars and academic theorists, who attempt to quantify and make into a science the art of stock portfolio investment, develop fresh ideas and theories. The crux of each of the above topics is to estimate both current and future stock values to make meaningful and potentially profitable investments. Nobel Prizes have been awarded to academic advances in different areas of portfolio theory. So why is any of this highly intellectual stuff a distraction to everyday investors? It's not an easy answer, but, in my opinion, the overcooking of basic investing by turning it into a scientific, mathematical, statistical endeavor is a distraction to the essence of disciplined saving and investing.

Modern portfolio theory was first attributed to the research of Professor Harry Markowitz, who did studies not only on performance and returns of optimum portfolios, but also incorporated risk parameters as part of his analysis. As a result of his research, and that of his collaborators, concepts such as diversification, asset allocation, and risk-adjusted return became axiomatic stock investment concepts. I will be addressing a few of those concepts a bit later, but for now, it's safe to say that Wall Street firms invest millions of dollars paying seasoned analysts and portfolio managers to apply these highly lauded principles in the course of providing investment products and services to their most powerful and valued clients.

The primary purpose of modern portfolio theory, and it's supporting methodologies, is to promote increased statistical probability that a selected security, or basket of securities, will deliver betters returns with lower risk than just investing in a standard benchmark, or simply throwing darts at a random list of stocks, bonds, or mutual funds. Most investors who feel they would benefit from the sophistication of Markowitz' work are in the category of large institutional investors, such as pension plans and endowment funds. To build a portfolio of several dozen stocks, to provide the broad coverage of many industries and investment categories, requires at least one million dollars, and sometimes much more. So it might not apply as readily to regular folks investing for retirement, or saving up for children's college education.

The purpose of this book does not include a discourse on advanced investment theories, but I felt it necessary because it provides value added to at least acknowledge that these concepts are readily available to Wall Street's clients and customers.

Let me add a brief word about the concept of risk-adjusted returns: even though some portfolios deliver lower returns than others, if a lower-return portfolio exposes an investor to less risk than a competing higher-return portfolio, it might be that the investor's risk-adjusted return could be higher. Today, modern portfolio encompasses a variety of theories involving risk/reward and optimum performing portfolios. Some of the more common theories include the capital asset pricing model (CAPM), efficient frontier, and the dividend discount model. None of these theories guarantee an investor will make a profit, but adhering to their disciplines generally, increases the probability of earning a profit.

The purpose of this book does not include expanded discussion of these well-accepted principles, often relied upon by analysts and portfolio managers. The reason that these principles collectively are listed as a misconception, from the perspective of the individual investor, is that they take a great deal of sophistication to implement. The individual investor would need to take courses, or do a great deal of individual study, to be able to understand and implement most of these theories. Thus, relying on these principles as an investment strategy without fully understanding their relevance to your personal financial goals would be like using a new vocabulary word in a speech without knowing its definition or part of speech. Just because something is a respected part of the industry doesn't necessarily make it is right for you.

Distraction #20: Alternative Investments / Nonconforming Assets

These terms could mean many different things to investors. Collectively, they refer to types of investments that are not the traditional Wall Street investments. The most common Wall Street investments are stocks, bonds, mutual funds, options, annuities, and, perhaps, life insurance. The most common types of alternative investments are hedge funds, commodities and futures, collateralized securities, precious metals, and in some cases, real estate. For purposes of this discussion, the terms alternative investments and nonconforming assets will refer to those investment types that meet two specific criteria. First, they are assets that do not have readily available standardized quotes, as do stocks, bonds, options, and mutual funds. The additional criterion is that of limited liquidity, meaning those assets that cannot readily be sold on a standardized exchange.

Based on these criteria, most commodities and futures contracts are considered traditional investments. These types of investments have similar real-time quotation systems during open market hours, and they are liquid in the sense that they can be sold instantaneously on a standardized exchange.

Nonconforming assets might include owning physical gold bullion, gold maple leaves, uncut diamonds, vacant land, or precious works of art. These kinds of investments take time to buy or sell, and their prices are not available on a standardized quotation system. Hedge funds evolved as a system of investing in nonconforming assets, and the hedge funds themselves were viewed as alternatives to traditional investments. The ownership format of most hedge funds is usually a limited partnership. The investors are the limited partners, and those managing the fund are referred to as the general partners. The general partners control everything, and the investors have little, if any, say in the selection or management of the investments. There is no readily available quotation system for valuing one's investment, and it often takes many months or several years to get one's money out of a hedge fund.

The misconception promoted by Wall Street is that hedge funds and other nonconforming assets can take on greater risk than can most traditional investments, and, in return, they deliver higher than average rates of return. Wall Street firms that offer hedge fund investments are careful to limit the investors to those with substantially higher net worths than average middle- class investors, and in that regard, disclose the higher risks involved. What many firms neglect to do is to make it extremely clear that in good times or bad, the investor may be prevented from liquidating the investment whenever desired. Investors may be required to wait several years, and even then, will only be allowed a limited window of opportunity during each twelve-month period to access their funds.

Studies made of the track records of various types of hedge funds, as well as other types of nonconforming investments, show that the long-term rates of return on most alternative investments are no higher than the general stock market. Naturally, there are short periods of time where any category can be shown to have superior returns. At the time this book is being written, it is certainly true that gold has had an impressive run over the last few years. Like any other impressive category of investment over the decades and centuries, everything levels out eventually. Many people who are getting on the gold bandwagon during the last few months have discovered that even Bellwether gold levels off at some point.

The real message of those touting alternative investments is that most of the alternative categories go up and down at differing times, similar to the stock market, but at different times. They view these categories as hedges against down trends in stocks and other traditional investments that are more closely correlated to each other. Certainly, there is merit in selecting a portion of your investments that hedge the downside of your stock investments.

The misconception on the part of investors is that they tend to overdo it. They don't just put a portion of their investment money in precious art or real estate or a hedge fund. They tend to get sold on the idea of how great such investments are, and then they bet the entire farm on the alternative categories. Eventually, they learn that traditional investments actually would have performed like the tortoise against the hare. Traditional investments would have done just as well, and actually a tad bit better than highly risky, nonconforming, alternative investments.

The answer to alternative investments is not cut and dry. There certainly is a place for nonconforming assets in the investment portfolios of all who wish to have them. The important thing is to know the role they play, and the amount of importance to place on such types of ownership. Again, it goes back to asking yourself what your financial goals are, what resources you have to allocate toward those goals, and what method(s) of investing are best suited to providing you with the rate or return necessary to accomplish your goals. If you wish to collect art, or coins, or stamps, or gold, know that you are using discretionary dollars for such items. You should understand that collectibles should be treated as hobbies, or as items of beauty that have value different from your savings and investments for attaining your future financial goals. They should be treated as extras, and not as substitutes for disciplined savings and investing plans.

Distraction #21: Derivatives

The accepted definition of a derivative, for investment purposes, is a security that can be traded on an organized exchange, and that relates or is derived from another type of investment instrument. Stock options are derivatives, and will be discussed below. In some respects, one could say that shares of stock themselves are derivatives. In the case of corporate common stocks, they are investment instruments derived from or related to the very companies (most of which are very large) of which they represent ownership shares. Almost all of these large corporations issue stock shares, each of which represents a fractional ownership of the company in question, and offer them for trading on one of the major stock exchanges.

For purposes of this book, the most common type of derivatives, of which most investors are familiar, are called stock options. Options on stock shares (often referred to as "puts and calls") are derived from the corporate shares of stock to which they relate. If you wish to invest in stocks, you either buy or sell the stocks themselves, or you can buy or sell options related to or underlying the corporate shares in question. The pricing of options is usually a mere fraction of the price of investing the shares directly.

Options were created so that you have the choice to either buy or sell a stock outright, or you can purchase an option giving yourself the right to either buy or sell the stock at a later time. In that sense, the option is derived from the underlying stock. An option related to a particular stock is almost always cheaper than the stock itself, and is, in most cases, deemed to be riskier than the underlying stock. The option being substantially less expensive than purchasing the stock itself, in most cases, puts the entire option investment at the risk of a complete loss.

This book is not the proper place to provide a full dissertation on options or other derivatives. Suffice to say that options and other derivatives can apply to stocks, to bonds, to mortgages, to commodities, and to numerous other types of securities. It can even be said that stocks themselves are a type of derivative.

When asked about my criteria for selecting stocks to include in mutual funds or portfolios that I manage, I always say that I choose companies that I would want to own if I had the wherewithal to buy them. Since I don't have that kind of money, I still act like a business owner and buy as many shares of such companies that I have the money to invest and responsibly diversify in accordance with my desired goals. Since I can't buy entire companies, I'm satisfied to buy the publicly traded shares of such companies.

So, we now come to the misconception. In a vast majority of cases, people will trade, meaning they will buy and sell derivatives as independent assets. This means they are trading derivatives as if they were the primary investment instruments, and not as a means of acquiring the underlying asset at either a cheaper cost, or with less probability of risk of loss. Thus, in all such cases where investors are trading in the derivatives themselves, they are, in reality, more like speculators than investors. Those who buy or sell derivatives are doing so with the hope and expectation that the prices of such instruments will rise or fall in their favor. They tend not to be interested in owning the underlying investment itself. This is pure speculation, gambling. Wall Street perpetuates this misconception by creating thousands of types of derivative instruments and offering them to institutions and individuals alike. The problem, the misleading part, is that they offer them as if these derivatives were true investments. In reality, they are nothing more than betting on red or black, on drawing to an inside straight, or attempts at rolling seven or eleven.

We, as investors, contribute to the misconception by encouraging Wall Street to offer these derivatives. Many investors who are sophisticated and knowledgeable about derivatives trade such instruments on a regular basis. They trade derivatives because their pricing is typically much cheaper than the underlying stocks or bonds from which they are derived. Such individuals feel they can leverage their investment dollars to capture greater upside gains, while investing only a fraction of what it would take to purchase the underlying stocks themselves. Unfortunately, there is a critical flaw in such thinking.

The misconception related to derivatives is that they involve extreme risk to the average investor not knowing all the possible outcomes that could occur. In far too many cases, the trade-off of potential gain is just not worth the risk involved. Because of the risk, it changes what would have been an investment in the stock itself into an act of pure speculation. Allow me to explain why.

If you make a traditional investment, such as buying shares of stock at the price of $50 per share, for example, and it goes down $5, you've lost 10% in value, but you still own the investment, now worth $45 per share instead of $50. If a dividend is paid, you still get the dividend. If you buy more shares at $45 per share, your yield on the dividend (assuming the dividend payments remain the same) actually increases. If the stock market goes back up over time, you are in a position to gain back the 10% loss, and potentially even more. In such instances, you're an investor.

The case of trading derivatives is different. With stock options for example, if you buy an option to purchase stock (commonly referred to as a "call" option), you now have the option to purchase, meaning you can "call it away" from its previous owner at $50 per share. You must make your decision to buy the stock at $50 per share before the time frame of the option expires. If the stock does not rise higher than $50 per share by the expiration date, your derivative (call option) will expire and be worthless. The derivative is not permanent and does not last forever. If, for example, you paid $3 per share for the derivative, and, in this case, the right to buy the stock at $50 per share, and instead of the stock rising above $50 per share it goes down by $5 to $45 per share at the expiration date, your $3 investment in the call-option derivative is reduced to $0.

It is true that cost of buying derivatives is usually only a fraction of the cost of buying the underlying stock outright, but the probability of losing the entire investment is dramatically increased. It is also true that many investors are tempted to invest the same dollar amount in the derivatives as they would in just buying the stock alone, thinking that for the same $50 investment, they can now potentially enjoy the upside gains of 15 or 16 shares (16 x $3 = $48), instead of the gain on only one share costing $50. The greedy temptation is based on the hope that if the stock price goes up by $5 per share, for example, from $50 to $55, instead of gaining $5 on one share, there is now the opportunity of gaining possibly $80 (16 x $5 = $80).

The danger and risk of this greedy thinking are just not worth it for the conservative investor. If the stock in this example does not rise from $50 to $55 within the time frame of the derivative, it is reduced to an all-or-nothing proposition, which is speculation. Statistical evidence has shown that most call options do not reach their target prices by the time they expire. It is my opinion that the potential reward is not worth the high probability risk of losing it all. Instead of being satisfied with a 10% gain versus the risk of 10% loss, the investor-turned- speculator is now willing to go after a 60% gain versus the potential of a 100% loss. This is not the thinking of an investor, but that of a speculator. In fact, here's a further reality check. In the above example, the stock would actually have to rise by $8 per share to $58 in to have a gain of $5 per share. The original $3 per share paid for the derivative actually shrinks to $0 by the time of expiration, so the stock would have to increase to at least $53 per share just to make up for the cost of buying the call option derivative.

In my opinion, taking these kinds of risks does not involve sound investing principles and is pure speculation, even if you are lucky enough to predict potential upward stock prices. If you are intrigued by the potential of using derivatives to create investment leverage, that's certainly your choice. Just don't be led into thinking that such programs are consistent with being an investor. They are more in the category of speculations, and Wall Street's misconception is that they do not identify them as such.

Distraction #22: Insider Information

Most people who trade in the stock market know that the use of "inside information" to gain an advantage to buy or sell securities carries stiff criminal penalties. Just ask Martha Stewart, who witnessed the inside of a cell for conduct she felt was inadvertent and not done to intentionally gain an advantage over other investors. Inside information is any material information about a publicly traded corporation to which the general public does not have access. If a person knows or has reason to know that the general public does not have access to the information upon which a decision to buy or sell a security is based, that constitutes illegal use of inside information.

It might be wise for a person to never take a stock "tip" at a cocktail party. If that tip, as innocent as the event might sound, turns out to be nonpublic, inside information, then the person relying on that knowledge gains an advantage not available to the general investing public.

The misconception here is that most individual investors feel they need a special advantage to be successful in the stock market. Wall Street brokers and firms have perpetuated this misconception for decades. If stock investing were presented in a more genuine, honest, and realistic manner, it would be made clear that most investors can reach their financial goals using sensible tools of stock investing. An investor should not need inside information. They simply need to know their goals and resources, and the tools available to them to achieve their goals based upon the resources they have available to allocate.

Another form of illegally seeking to have an unfair advantage in the trading of stocks or other securities is simply referred to as market manipulation. I have not set this out as a separate distraction, because the nature of the illegality is pretty much the same. If a savvy investor figures out a way to get a better deal, or reduce risk to zero by getting special treatment when buying or selling their investments, the regulatory agencies deem it to be illegal. Investing is the right of all people who wish to play the game. Everyone with resources and the desire to participate is entitled to a level playing field, limited only by the amount of resources they have, and the amount of time put into researching publicly available investment information.

Market manipulation often occurs by the spreading of false rumors (I guess not all rumors are false) about a particular company, or its stock, or another type of traded security. When dealing with smaller companies, perhaps a very wealthy individual or large institution will attempt to buy or sell such huge quantities of the related corporate stock, so as to influence the direction and amount of price change of that stock. The person or entity doing this manipulation generally will receive an excessive profit if successful. Sometimes the desired result can occur by spreading rumors about the company.

As a final note on this topic, the use of inside information, or attempts to manipulate prices, is illegal for a reason. Knowing the secret events, plans, opportunities, and pending disasters known only by inside managers and directors of companies in which we invest is something everybody feels they would like to know about. If the company wants the public to know about it, they'll publish the information through normal channels. If not, they want it to remain secret, and dissemination of rumors about company secrets by unsavory individuals disrupts the normal investing process engaged in by the majority of the investing public. Any excessive buying or selling by persons who know or think they know such secrets is taking an unfair advantage over the rights of the general investing public to have a level playing field.

Distraction #23: "We'd Like to Offer You Some Research."

There is no such thing as a "free lunch." Actually, there is, because that phrase itself is a misconception. What's important here is that you generally don't get something for nothing. The idea of someone cold-calling on the phone and offering research about certain types of stocks comes about from two separate perspectives. In most instances, this occurs when Wall Street firms call up institutional investors, and even other Wall Street firms, offering research in the form of analysts' opinions to other professionals in the field. Lately, this type of research is also offered to individual investors by the brokerage houses that hold their portfolio accounts.

In some cases, firms will charge a fee for their research, and in other cases, the research is offered free of charge to encourage buying and selling that generates commissions. In reality, research is not often given away without some commitment or compensation required from the recipient. The offering firm might require the recipient to open up a trading account, or the recipient might be required to make a certain number of stock or bond trades, or maintain a margin borrowing account. Salaries for stock analysts are usually quite high, and some type of compensation is required for the firm not to lose money in that department.

The fact that there may or may not be a charge for stock research is not the crux of the misconception. Research offered to institutional traders and individual traders alike usually comes with some form of bias or slant. Research from the major wire houses is usually thorough, informative, and factual. But, in most cases, it comes with an angle, slant, or motive to either promote a purchase or to promote a sale. It is rarely completely objective, because it always comes with some kind of recommendation— buy, hold, sell, overweight, underweight. If you own the stock, and the recent audited numbers are bad, you must sell. If you don't own the stock, and the recent numbers are good, you must buy, etc.

The research comes with a recommendation for action. Action means buy or sell. Occasionally, the recommendation is to "hold," but hold in stock analyst language means sell. Why? Because, in most cases, a "hold" recommendation follows a previous recommendation of "buy" or "strong buy." Some of us skeptics might ask what the difference is between "buy" and "strong buy"? Does one mean buy just a little bit, and the other means buy a whole bunch? The distinction doesn't even make any sense. Back to the point: if an analyst's research recommendation is to "hold," it usually follows a previous recommendation of "buy"; so, in essence, it is a downgrade of the stock. By implication, it is a recommendation to sell.

In summary, an offer to provide research is an offer to provide a subjective recommendation based upon analyst's research that is in the best interest of the firm providing the "free lunch" to generate movement.

Firms have a variety of motives for wanting to be the provider of the information to customers and clients. Firstly, they offer the research on a trial basis, hoping that if you like the research, you will want to receive it on a regular basis and will be inclined to work with them. However, after the introductory sample of the research reports they provide, if you want to receive it on a regular basis, you will have to pay for it. Their research is a source of revenue to the firm, and if you want to receive the juicy tidbits provided therein, you will have to pay for it. There is no free lunch.

Secondly, the research is slanted or biased in one way or another. On many occasions, the firm doing the research makes a market in the stock in question. This means that the firm is a buyer and a seller of the stock of the company upon which they have done this extensive research. This means that the firm deliberately takes the opposite side of numerous transactions of buying and selling of the stock in question by the firm's clients. If a customer wants to sell his shares, the firm is the buying entity. If a customer wants to buy shares, they—the firm—are the seller to its own client. There is always a bid-ask spread when customers buy or sell shares, and because the firm itself is always on the opposite side of the transactions involving stocks for which it provides research to its clients, the firm is always making the bid-ask spread from those purchases and sales. The firm has a clear motive to stimulate interest by its clients, in certain stocks, by providing research information to stimulate fees from the bid-ask spread.

Thirdly, many firms serve as investment bankers for the companies to whom it provides research. Investment bankers charge huge fees for their IPO and secondary placement underwritings. Research stimulates interest and a following for new stock offerings, so there is a motive to produce reports with a promising outlook so as to invite investors to place orders for these fresh offerings. They have a motive to want to move out all the new shares, and to move them quickly. In fact, if they can create a huge demand for their underwritings, they earn additional fees. Part of their underwriting arrangements usually involves the investment banking firms receiving a percentage of the shares of the new company. They personally benefit from excess demand, because their shares will increase in value due to the demand created during their underwriting promotion.

Fourthly, most research firms are also broker-dealers or stock clearing firms. These firms make a good portion of their profits from the activity of making a market in many of the stocks publicly traded on the exchanges or over the NASDAQ. Even if they are not involved in an initial or secondary public offering of a particular stock, there is a good chance that the firm makes a market in trading that stock. By making a market, we mean that whenever their clients want to buy a particular stock, the firm itself has the stock in its inventory, and serves as the seller to the client. Then, when a client wants to sell that stock, they serve as the buyer of the stock. Therefore, stocks in which they are market makers, they earn a commission for whenever they buy or sell from their own clients.

In summary, the purpose of offering research is a subtle way of promoting the purchase and sale of stocks the firm follows, underwrites, and in which it makes a market. In recent years, ethical rules have emerged to inhibit firms from being overly aggressive in tying their research to their trading activities. So-called "firewalls" are established at firms to separate their research departments from their investment banking and from their brokerage activities. But promotional activities are by no means prohibited, and the offering of research to woo new clients is clearly pursued with the intent of creating new relationships with clients having a propensity for frequent buying and selling of stocks.

Distraction #24: Good News / Bad News

There's financial news every day. There has to be because that's how news agencies and media stay in business. But does that mean that Wall Street firms and their clients should react to every piece of news that hits the wires?

News should be relevant to an individual investor's goals before actions are taken, and devoid of emotionally driven reactions. Does a crisis with the economy of a European country require that an American corporate employee holding a portfolio of dividend-paying stocks— building a nest egg for retirement— run for hills and turn all holdings into cash or convert to gold? Sure the bad news about a foreign country could trickle down and affect interest rates or the price of oil at the local level, but such information is mainly a distraction from the long-range goal of systematically saving and investing for one's retirement.

Likewise, we need to take the same level of caution when the news is good. Should the announcement that XYZ technology company has just released a new form of wireless technology the size of a fingernail that will revolutionize the entertainment industry dictate that you should reposition your entire portfolio? Is it a good idea to always try to "keep up with the Joneses"? The message in this is that the average investor should try to be disciplined, sticking to a fundamentally sound portfolio that is stable in both good times and bad.

Professional investment advisors are not keeping their clients and customers best interests in mind if they constantly encourage them to react and take action with every piece of earth-shaking news that comes down the pike. Again, this goes back to the previously discussed issue of investors receiving a commission for every trade you make and using news and information as a leverage tool to encourage you to buy and sell regularly.

Let's face it, good news makes us ecstatic; bad news makes us depressed. It is my view that there is no place for these extreme emotions when managing a business or managing your investments. Such emotions should be reserved for our social relationships, for romance, for raising our children, for dealing with health issues. It even makes sense to have these emotions at the casino, or when waiting to see if your lottery ticket is a winner.

As an underlying theme of this book, it has been stressed that saving and investing for your financial goals should be a consistent endeavor, sticking to your plan. You should make every attempt to avoid distractions that tempt you to stray from your course of action. Daily sound bites and news releases invite us to react, and distract us from using the wonderful tools that Wall Street has to offer. Mainly, such distractions tend to make us abandon the sensible investment tools that are readily available to help us be successful in achieving our long-range financial goals. Simply stated, reacting to every piece of news, good or bad, is like being a rabbit, zigzagging back and forth, never making up its mind which way to go. What we investors ought to do, and what Wall Street should promote, is staying the course like the turtle, who keeps plodding along, nice and straight, and eventually crosses the finish line first.

Distraction #25: Earnings Announcements / Earnings Surprises

Wall Street analysts regularly publish estimates of the upcoming revenues and earnings of the numerous public corporations that they follow. They use a variety of tools and data to come up with their estimates. Sometimes they gather information by interviewing corporate management, and other times they look at published data, and extrapolate historical trends into the future. It also occasionally occurs that the management of some corporations will issue forward-looking press releases, stating their internal estimates of coming years' revenues and earnings.

What should be made clear is that these forecasts of future corporate earnings and revenues results are just estimates from Wall Street analysts. Even though they are often educated guesses, they are just guesses. Analysts' estimates of what company earnings will be are by no means official. They are not required to be filed with the SEC or any other regulatory agency. Since they are guesses, the actual earnings reported by many companies will be different from the estimates—sometimes higher, sometimes lower.

Whenever the real numbers are different from the "consensus" estimates, Wall Street calls them "earnings surprises." Why they are called surprises is not clear to me. Since estimates are not intended to be the real numbers, isn't it reasonable and foreseeable that the true numbers will be a surprise? Isn't it just as much a surprise if the real number comes out exactly as the estimate as to when it comes out different? But Wall Street calls it a surprise, and the stock market rewards or punishes the real numbers, depending on whether the real earnings come out higher or lower than the estimates.

Two problems occur with stock trading that relies on earnings surprises. When the true results are higher than the estimates, it's viewed as an upside surprise, and when the results are less than the estimates, it's called a downside surprise. The first problem is that even the smallest surprise—say just a penny or two per share above or below the estimates—may trigger a dramatic move in the stock price by stock traders who feed on earnings announcements. It is mind-boggling to observe large stock moves when, for example, analysts' estimates forecast that XYZ stock will enjoy upcoming earnings report of $.50 earnings per share, and when the actual report is released, the actual earnings were only $.49 per share.

What is more baffling is that this $.49 per share earnings might have been, for example, more than a 10% increase over the prior year's earnings for the same time period. The company still made more money than the prior year, yet the stock price gets punished by the stock market for "missing the estimates."

The same market reaction can also occur on the upside when a company beats the earnings estimates, sometimes by just a small amount. As stated earlier, estimates are just estimates. The single stock or wholesale market response to surprises in earnings estimates speaks volumes to volatility and the importance of long-term investing. Nothing stated in this book is likely to change how stock traders react to earnings surprises, but it should help you to better understand Wall Street and educate you as to certain misconceptions about what is good and what is bad in terms of stock performances. I want you to know the right questions to ask. If your broker calls you up and says, "Hey, Jimmy, we need to dump five hundred shares of XYZ stock. It underperformed based on its quarterly estimates." I want you to be in a position to investigate and make an independent decision. Ignore the fact that the stock didn't meet the estimate and ask how it actually performed in comparison to its previous value. If it went up, who cares by how much? If it went down, by how much?

The message to long-term investors, those who wish to use the many sensible tools Wall Street has to offer, is that the publishing of "earnings surprises" is indeed a distraction to those with a disciplined, consistent approach to investing. Recognizing such distractions, and making an effort not to let them cause you to stray from your plan, or to falter in your discipline, will result in a much better probability of achieving your investment goals.

Distraction #26: Guaranteed Investments

Let's start with a bold statement: in reality, **there is no such thing as a guaranteed investment**. There is no investment on the planet in which absolutely nothing can go wrong. The soundest, safest investment known to our society is the purchase of US treasury bills, notes, and bonds. There is nothing safer available to us. They are backed by the full faith and credit of the United States of America. Everything else is a step down. But even treasuries are not guaranteed. Even treasuries carry a certain amount of investment risk.

If you hold a treasury security until maturity, you are as certain as humanly possible to receive the promised interest payments along the way, and the promised principal investment returned at the time of maturity. So what are the risks? They are aplenty.

If interest rates increase and you wish to sell off the Treasury note or bond prior to its date of maturity, the value will be less than the face amount of the security. Yes, you will lose some money. These types of risks are called interest rate risk and liquidity risk. On the other hand, if interest rates fall while you hold the note or bond, the value of the bond you hold will actually increase in value. So you might sell it at a profit. That's great, but if you want to invest in another treasury instrument right away, you will get less interest on your investment because it's a period of lower interest rates. This type of risk is called reinvestment risk.

What about other so-called guaranteed investments offered by Wall Street firms? Let's start with life insurance policies. If you own a $100,000 term life insurance policy, for example, we know two things for sure. First, we know you are someday going to die. Second, if you make all the required premium payments and die of natural causes within the term of the policy, the insurance company guarantees to pay $100,000 to your beneficiaries.

What's wrong with that? The main problem arises if the insurance company becomes insolvent before you die. The guarantee is only as good as the strength and honesty of the company giving the guarantee. This might also occur with certain annuities issued by life insurance companies. Many annuity policies guarantee payment of a certain amount of money every year for the rest of your life, beginning after you reach a certain age. Again, there are still things that can go wrong. The company might fold, or the person supposedly entitled to receive the guaranteed payments could be accused of fraud in the application process.

Many times we purchase products that have money-back guarantees. Even though we are primarily dealing with purchases of consumer products, the issues related to guarantees is the same. A guarantee is only as good as the firm or entity giving the guarantee.

In the world of investments, investors occasionally encounter an investment program where the investment managers guarantee a certain rate of return. A certain famous person, now languishing in jail, promised his investors a 10% return annually for as long as he managed their investments. The promised or "guaranteed" return continued for many years, until the Ponzi scheme nature of the program was discovered and revealed. Guarantees and promises are only as good as the person or entity giving the guarantee. And, if it sounds too good to be true, it is!

In some cases, the Wall Street account executives and advisors who are selling such guaranteed products are themselves misled.

In presenting such investment programs to their clients, they, too, rely on the good reputation and past performance of the investment programs they offer to clients. Once they get burned, and find themselves liable for losses they offered in good faith, they, too, eventually come to understand that there is no such thing as a guaranteed investment.

Members of the investing public, and the Wall Street representatives who service them, should cooperate in their understanding that investment programs claiming the label of "guaranteed" ought to be looked at carefully. Perhaps they should be avoided altogether.

Instead of looking for guaranteed investments, perhaps it is wiser to look for investments that have the highest probability of performing as well as possible, given the economic conditions of the time, your goals, and the assets you have to allocate.

Distraction #27: Financial Plans / Portfolio Reviews

It is quite common, and even required practice at many Wall Street firms, that investment advisors and portfolio managers provide their clients with reviews of their portfolio holdings on a periodic basis. In addition to reviewing any changes in their risk tolerance (to be discussed in greater detail below), advisers want to go over the progress of the investments over the prior year or past six months. In many cases, they advise their clients to have a financial plan, and the purpose of the review is to determine if the clients' portfolios are performing consistently with the goals of their financial plan.

What could be wrong or misconceiving about having a financial plan, and then reviewing its progress on a regular basis? The answer is pretty straightforward. Most periodic reviews provide the opportunity to point out weaknesses in your investment portfolio, real or not, to promote commissioned-based buying and selling. From the Wall Street professional's point of view, this gives an opportunity to suggest replacing some of the poorly performing investments with new selections. From the perspective of a savvy client, this seemingly beneficial exercise creates a variety of doubts.

Isn't it the advisor who put the portfolio together and who is now pointing out the weaknesses? Isn't the advisor suggesting selling some of the securities and replacing them with others? If the professional advisor is a traditional Wall Street broker, isn't the broker going to earn fees or commissions for suggesting this selling and buying to improve the portfolio? So the investment professional is going to make money on pointing out the weaknesses he is partially responsible for creating. Clients could easily be suspicious that the main reason for such periodic reviews is for commission-based account executives to have an opportunity to generate more fees in the process of "improving" their portfolio.

Is providing formal financial plans for clients equally misleading? There is an entire industry composed of certified financial planners. The investment professionals involved in that sector of Wall Street professionals are highly respected, and spend numerous hours keeping up on their education and staying current with developments in their industry.

The misconception is not with the advisors who offer planning services; rather it is in the nature of how financial plans are presented. They are presented in such complex and overly elaborate formats that they are too confusing for most people to understand. Many of them are very costly, and are top-heavy with a table of contents, index, and numerous charts and graphs requiring an economist and tax specialist to explain. Some clients might be suspicious that such elaborate plans are presented with other purposes in mind. Again, the misconception might be that the elaborate financial plans are really presented with a motive to sell clients a variety of other products, of which they may be less familiar than stocks, bonds, and mutual funds. Consider a few simple questions if presented with a financial plan: How much does the person who presented you with the plan know about your short- and long-term financial goals? How much time have they spent discussing the resources you have available toward accomplishing your financial goals? How much in their plan reflects the answers to the first two questions?

In section three of this book, I offer you a truly simplified retirement plan approach that can be used to help you identify the answers to very important questions before embarking on an investing strategy. The true point of financial planning is to arrive at a stated amount of money that will be needed at some point in the future through a combination of realistic savings and sound investing processes. Understanding your plan will empower you to critically assess how well your investments are performing and whether or not action is needed.

Distraction #28: "What Is Your Risk Tolerance? Are You Aggressive or Conservative?"

Some of the better financial planning firms and investment advisory firms offer all potential clients a questionnaire that presents a series of "what if" questions that help determine the client's tolerance for risk, and for potential losses. After completing the questionnaire, whether it is in writing or verbal, the advisor feels better equipped to select investments that tend to be more conservative (lower risk) or more aggressive (high risk).

This process is deemed to be good practice by firms truly concerned with selecting the best potential investments for their clients. In fact, the better firms will ask their clients to complete such questionnaires on a periodic basis, at least as frequently as every three or four years. It is commonly felt on Wall Street that as time goes by clients become less risky and more conservative. This might be a function of increasing age, or it might be due to changing economic conditions that might make aggressive investments riskier than they were during strong economic periods.

Everything about this process sounds wise and proper. In fact, there is nothing presented in this book that will dare suggest that such inquiries should not be made. There is a strong mandate in the investment industry that firms are required to "know their client" before offering investment choices to them. So where's the misconception in this process?

As has been concluded with some of the previous concepts, this might be one of giving lip service to a sound and reasonable process, and then ignoring the findings. In how many cases has a high-net-worth client been evaluated to be conservative, and yet the firm places the same investor in a hedge fund, an energy development partnership, or some other illiquid private placement because the client has the financial ability to "afford" this type of investment? A low tolerance for risk not only includes conservative investments, but also those investments that are fairly liquid.

Risk-tolerance profile questionnaires are valuable tools for investment firms to know and understand their clients' needs. The problem is twofold. First, there is the issue of whether the firms adhere to the conclusions drawn from the questionnaires. In far too many instances, the advisor or broker offers investments that sound good when presented, but, in reality, are juxtaposed to the client's needs or goals.

The second problem is probably just as big as the first one. I contend that the risk tolerance questionnaires ask the wrong questions and do not address the real information the financial advisor should have. Typical questionnaires ask whether a client can live with short-term or even long-term reductions in the value of his or her portfolio. Why should anybody ever say yes to that question? Once again, this insinuates a message from Wall Street that every client should be looking at the price of their holdings every day, maybe every minute of every day, to see if their stocks or other investments are up or down. This is just not how sound investing should operate. Moreover, it suggests that the firm has some control over whether or not they can indeed pick a plan that will avoid short- or long-term reductions. If that were the case, wouldn't everyone option for never having any reduction?

Why not ask the question more directly: How frequently do you look at the prices of your investments? If the answer is every day, then the advisor has a clue that he or she is dealing with a speculator. If the client looks at statements once a month, now we are talking about a potentially long-term investor.

Why not ask questions similar to the following: Do you understand there is a difference between the general stock market going up and down, as influenced by the state of the economy, and your investments fluctuating, either the same as the general market or differently from the general market? Which would concern you the most? The answers to these types of questions provide real information about the risk tolerance of the investor.

I also feel that knowing your client should include questions like: How much money do you want to accumulate, and over what period of time? How much money do you have to start with? How much additional funding do you plan to add to your account during the time you are building up your estate? The answers to these types of questions will allow investment advisors to "know their clients."

Placing labels on investors as conservative or aggressive is not sufficient to help them reach their financial goals. No reasonable person should answer yes to a question that asks whether they can tolerate losses. Nobody in their right mind should want to tolerate losses. If someone came up to you and asked, "Excuse me, are you comfortable with failure?" "Of course not." So why does Wall Street present a questionnaire that sets up its customers and clients for failure? It doesn't make sense, unless that's what Wall Street expects.

Distraction #29: Regression Toward the Mean

As the pendulum swings, on average it is motionless. Regression to the mean, or convergence toward the mean, is just another way of saying "the law of averages." Most people don't realize this concept works if used in the right perspective. The idea is that if you look at historical stock prices, and then calculate an average rate of return over a certain period of time, that average return will continue over time. It makes no difference that today stock prices are either above or below that average number.

To avoid misunderstanding, the law of averages does not say that whatever the average number is will be the resulting number most of the time. Average numbers are derived from the fact that numbers occur both above and below the computed average number. So for example, let's say you read a statistic that the average rate of return for the general stock market was 9.5% per year over the last seventy-five years. This is just an example, so that number is hypothetical. What we must tell you is that even if true, the rate of return of 9.5% is not necessarily the rate of return you will experience next year, or for any year. It merely states that 9.5% is a "mean" or average statistical return, around which all the actual returns revolved during the seventy-five-year period.

Regression to the mean, or the law of averages, suggests that future returns of the stock market, assuming the markets face the same assortment of variables in future years, will also revolve around that same statistical average rate of return. In any one year, or even a group of years, the actual returns will be higher or lower than that average number.

Where the misconception arises, both from Wall Street's and individual investor's perspectives, is when there are a few years where the stock market returns are consistently above, or below, the long-term average. Does that mean the next year will have the opposite results to average out? A better way to illustrate this question is dealing with flips of a coin. We all know that given a large number of flips, there's a high probability that we will get an equal number of heads and tails. Yet, in a short number of flips, let's say twenty flips, it is possible to get, for example, fifteen tails and five heads. Does that mean the next ten flips will all be heads? Of course not. Each flip has a fifty-fifty probability of being either heads or tails. It may take another twenty-five or thirty flips to regress to the average results of half tails and half heads overall, maybe even more.

The message here is that regression to the mean, as it relates to stock market returns, applies over longer periods of time. The results of a downside stock market, or a highly volatile stock market, or a strong upside market can vary dramatically from the long-term average rate of return of the general market. This has been shown to be true during several periods in the history of the stock market. For example, the 1990s was a period of excessively high rates of return. The effects of regression to the mean required a long enough time frame to allow the principle to work.

Short-term trading and speculation will generally not benefit from the concept of the law of averages. Many stock traders rely on a principle that the "trend is your friend." This suggests that when looking at a stock chart—despite whether it is trending up or down—that you should rely on the current trend. This is another way of saying that you can rely on a short-term version of regression to the mean. This could result in dramatic losses by a short-term trader. As we've said, the speculation game is generally won only by a few. There are too many variables that impact the short-term stock market.

The reality is that short-term, unforeseen variables cancel each other out over longer periods of time. In the short term, all the good news and bad news is mostly unforeseen, e.g., a political crisis in a foreign country, natural disasters of all kinds, economic mismanagement both domestically and abroad, etc. These events all interrupt trends in the short-term stock market. Over the long haul, we all know that history repeats itself.

We see political changes in president and congress; we see increases and decreases with interest rates and inflation; and with prices of gold, oil, and other commodities. None of these events are new, and they all recur. Awareness and knowledge of average rates of return on stock investments over the long term are justified. Employing the law of averages, or regression to the mean, for periods of thirty or forty years, or even longer, can help in making realistic investment decisions. They can even help in forming realistic expectations with any person's investment plan.

Distraction #30: Constantly Checking the Prices of Our Stocks

We all do it. We can't help it. Is it because the information is so readily available on a real-time basis? Is it because Wall Street professionals themselves are constantly doing it that it entices us to feel like we're better informed if we constantly keep track of our favorite stocks?

In no other investment category do investors have their smartphones and computers programmed to constantly tell us how much money we are making or losing during every moment of the day Monday through Friday. If you invest in real estate, are you calling your real estate broker every morning for an appraisal before you have your first cup of coffee? Do we call our life insurance agent on a regular basis to find out if it's okay to go ahead and die, and whether the kids will get the amount of the policy? How about calling the jeweler every afternoon to see if the engagement ring is worth as much this week as when you received it from your fiancé? Can't you hear the cocktail party talk now? "Hey, Joe, my art collection went up by a hundred grand this week, how did your antique sculpture collection do?" It would be sheer craziness. Checking our stock prices every day is sheer craziness.

So why do we all do it? Can we put all the blame on Wall Street and the media? Maybe we are just as much to blame. We have allowed ourselves to be programmed into thinking that we are actually making money or losing money if the quoted prices of our securities change. That is nonsense. What I have been trying to make you, my readers, understand is that it's all about the cash flow. That's what investors deal with: the rental income, the interest income, the dividend income, and whether it is received on a regular basis. A person who owns a retail business measures value on how much is sold each day or each month against the expenses paid out each day or each month. What's left over is the profit, and that's how business people look at their investments.

Only when you actually go to sell your stocks, or buy more stocks, should you be seriously concerned with the price quotations. It's true, if you don't like the current price you might delay your transactions hoping for lower prices if you are a buyer, or higher prices if you are a seller. I have commented in other places my view of buying or selling too frequently or without a disciplined plan. But it is important to learn and assimilate that the primary time to be focused on price changes of stocks is when you are planning a transaction.

If it is not the time to buy or sell in your particular circumstance, don't keep checking your stock prices. The only rational time, if you are not planning any upcoming transactions, is to look at your monthly brokerage statement and objectively fashion review your holdings and the overall condition of your portfolio in comparison to prior time periods. In this fashion, you'll get a feeling of whether or not your holdings, as a group, are working for you, and progressing in the right direction. You will then use this opportunity to determine if you need corrective action. If you were working with an investment professional, you would be wise, at that time, to contact him or her, if you see a problem.

I believe that the suggestions I've just made are consistent with the way rational investors handle other investment categories. Those who invest in real estate and small family businesses act more objectively and rationally. Even serious collectors of art, antiques, stamps, coins, and gems conduct themselves in a more businesslike fashion than most of us trading stocks on Wall Street. All investments and business ventures carry risk, but I know of no other category that generates more stress for the average participant than stock market participants. That does not have to be. One step toward minimizing stress and worry for those who wish to be true stock investors will be to stop the continuous checking of their stock prices.

Wall Street symbolizes American capitalism and our free market economy probably more than any other institution.

For many Americans, especially those who wish to use one or more of the investing tools Wall Street has to offer, it is difficult to understand how Wall Street works. For many of us, it can be mind-boggling, fraught with confusion and distractions.

A major theme of this section is identifying some of the numerous misconceptions and distractions promulgated by Wall Street firms and the media. It is my feeling that if we could have the strength and discipline to ignore such distractions, we would sleep better and be more successful with our investing.

There are numerous investing tools available to us all, but we are often deterred from their usage by the various distractions and misconceptions discussed in this section.

These distractions and misconceptions are a cross-section or sampling of the numerous myths and expressions often associated with stock market investing, which mask or deter the average person from the process of true investing.

Here are some of the themes we identified in this part of the book:

1. Differentiating between investing and speculating.

2. Investment recommendations that are motivated by the generation of excessive fees for investment professionals.

3. Encouraging frequent term trading as opposed to long-term investing.

4. Chasing excessively high rates of return not required to meet your financial goals.

5. Making "bragging" rights, and doing better than your neighbor, more important than steady cash returns.

6. Placing unnecessary importance on predicting the future movement of stock prices, the stock market, and the economy.

7. Making investors think that knowing "why" the market or certain stocks went up or down is going to improve their investment results.

8. Continual emphasis on changing prices of stocks and other securities.

9. The idea that the opinion of a Wall Street professional, or even a friend or relative, about stock movements is going to make a difference.

10. Highly sophisticated statistical models and unique investing styles (including touted work of Nobel laureates) have not necessarily produced better results than sound, common-sense investing.

11. The "herd" mentality of the stock market in the short term, versus the power of long- term investing in financially sound companies.

12. The common technique of emphasizing "complexity" and hard-to-explain formulas and computerized investments that will "automatically" produce superior results.

13. Failure to treat Wall Street investing with discipline.

14. Failure to treat Wall Street investing similar to running a business.

In addition to the common themes among the list of distractions, it was emphasized that these and other distractions are perpetuated both by Wall Street professionals, and by investors themselves. This section was not designed to assign blame to any individual, or institution, or participant. All facets of Wall Street feed on the traditions and types of communications that have been part of the fabric for over one hundred years.

For those who participate in the Wall Street process, awareness of distractions or obstacles to sound investing might help some investors to be more focused and disciplined in pursuing their financial goals and aspirations.

It is certainly my hope that you now feel better informed as to some of the more common distractions and misconceptions that exist on Wall Street. I hope you will take this information with you as we move to the next section to discuss some of the more powerful tools Wall Street offers to you.

SECTION 2:

TEN POWERFUL TOOLS OF INVESTING

After serving for many years as an investment advisor and stockbroker, and after reading numerous books on the topic of investing and portfolio management, I have concluded that there are several powerful investment tools, ten to be exact, available to assist us all in making investments on Wall Street. Most investors are unaware how basic and straightforward these investment tools can be. They often overlook, ignore, underutilize, or simply just don't know about them. The underlying theme in presenting these basic yet highly effective tools is treating investing more like a sound business rather than a game of chance or speculation. Additionally, the use of any or all of these tools should help investors feel empowered, more in control of their financial future, and less stressed.

In this section of the book, I will present ten powerful investing tools that, when used separately or in combination, can yield positive and realistic results over the long term. Keep in mind that none of these ideas are new concepts or fresh theories, nor are these the only investment tools that are available to yield successful results for dedicated investors. I have chosen these tools to present because ten is a nice round number and, more importantly, these tools have certain common and complementary traits based on common sense and capability of practical application by anyone and everyone who chooses to use them.

The reason these tools are powerful is not that the people who use them are going to beat the market or set the world on fire. They are powerful because they allow investors who use them to better understand and control the outcome of their endeavors. Anybody who engages in securities investments knows that no single person can control the economy or the ups and downs of the stock market. A central theme of this book is to try to educate and empower investors as to what they can control and what they cannot control in the universe of securities investments. These particular ten tools represent choices that investors can make, that they can control, and that increase the probability of achieving outcomes that they want and expect.

One additional comment before getting into the tools themselves: in almost every instance of using the various tools in question, an investor will generally not observe anything dramatic out of the gate. In the case of each tool, whether used separately or in combination with one another, the success, power, and gratification will only be observed after an extended period of time. The investor will have to give these tools time to do their work. In other words, there is no quick fix or secret recipe, and you should be leery of anyone who tells you differently. With any sound investment strategy, investors will have to exercise patience and discipline before they see the reward of their efforts.

I'm happy to report that even though it takes time to see the full power of these tools from a financial perspective, there is an immediate upside. Allow me to explain: What are some of the more common emotions we tend to experience about our financial investments? Doubt? Uncertainty? Lack of understanding? Lack of control? Do any of these sound familiar? And they all lead to added stress and frustration, right? Well, what if you knew not only how to identify what your financial goals were, but had the ability to create a road map for yourself and understand the tools and process that were going to get you there? These ten powerful investment tools empower you to understand how to make your money work for you. Moreover, as many of us already have our money invested in some capacity or another, understanding these tools will allow you to ask questions and make adjustments based upon your individualized goals. No more uncertainty; no more doubt; no more lack of control. Just less stress and less frustration.

I want to preface the introduction of these tools by reminding you that it is not my intention to encourage you to implement all of these tools at once, but rather to identify your goals and then decide which tool or tools best serve you in accomplishing your goals. Once I have introduced you to the tools, the next section will help you to identify your personal financial goals and plan.

POWERFUL TOOL #1: COMPOUNDING OVER TIME

There is no single investment tool more powerful than compounding. This means either the compounding of interest on your savings, or the compounding of the average rate of return on your securities investments. Most people understand the concept of compounding, but for those who do not, the simplest way to explain it is that compounding means earning interest on interest. This means that you not only earn a rate of return on your investment, but, over time, you also earn a rate of return on your rate of return, over the entire time frame of your investment. Thus, compounding over time. For this investment tool to work properly, you should continually reinvest the interest or dividends you receive. Both the original investment and the interest or dividends grow, usually at the average rate of return over the life of the investment.

Compounding is not effective, however, if you don't give it time to do its work. Time cannot come into play unless we exhibit patience and discipline. Compounding over time becomes even more powerful if we combine it with the tool of continuous contributions. Continuous contributions will be addressed in the next tool, but, for now, let's get a good appreciation for the tool of compounding over time.

And in the same vein, time by itself does nothing for an investor, unless allowed to work in tandem with compounding. One way to illustrate the power of compounding over time is to repeat a well-known story frequently told in the form of an exaggeration to show the impact of compounding over time. If the resident native tribe, which legend has it sold the island of Manhattan to the Dutch colonists for the modest sum of $24 in tokens and trinkets, could have invested that amount in an interest-bearing savings account, compounding at the average conservative rate of 4% annually from 1646 until today, then after approximately four hundred years of compounding, the resulting sum would be just under $87 million. More impressively, if the average compounded rate of return would have been just one percent higher, at 5% annually, the sum would be a whopping

$3.5 billion today. Yes, this is a long time, but it was just $24, and hopefully, you can see how powerful the tool of compounding can be.

We can also see from this example that not only is time important to allow compounding to do its work, but when a person is trying to invest and save for a particular purpose, in most cases, the more time, the better. If people who seek to invest and save can give their invested money time to compound and grow, the rewards can be tremendous.

Let's look at another example perhaps a little more realistic than the Manhattan story. Suppose a person, age forty-five, receives an inheritance of $200,000 and decides to save and invest the full amount for the next twenty years, to be used to fulfill future financial goals at the time of retirement at age sixty-five. Let's also assume the person will earn on average 6% annually and does not spend any of the funds during the twenty-year period. If our investor can let the full amount compound without making any withdrawals until age sixty-five (assuming that taxes, fees, and other expenses are paid from other sources), the tool of compounding will do its work for our investor. The amount of the fund will grow to approximately $640,000 by the end of the twenty-year saving and compounding period.

Let's make a couple of variations. Many investments compound more frequently than once annually. Using the above example, if the same sum of $200,000, earning 6%, actually compounded on a monthly basis, which means it compounds at the rate of .5% per month (equals 6% annually), the sum will grow even larger. At the end of the twenty-year period, when our investor reaches age sixty-five, the resulting sum will be approximately $660,000.

And one additional variation can make an even more dramatic difference. Again using the above example, if we increase the annual rate of return by just 1% annually, thus compounding at the rate of 7% annually, this same $200,000, invested for a period of twenty years, the resulting total would make all that waiting worthwhile. At the end of twenty years, the resulting total would increase to approximately $807,000.

Truth be told, not everyone has a lump sum of $200,000, or any other large sum to begin a saving and investing program. As a final example related to this powerful tool, let's assume a bit more modest beginning of the saving and investing process, while factoring in a disciplined, habitual approach to building your retirement nest egg.

In this scenario, let's assume our saver-investor is a recent college graduate who was fortunate enough, during tough economic conditions, to find a decent-paying job. This new member of the workforce decides to take on a doubly difficult task of steadily paying off student loans and also setting aside money to supplement the retirement plan that her employer provides for her.

She decides that no matter what her monthly student loan payment is, she will set aside enough money to make an annual contribution of $5,000 into an individual retirement account (IRA). She is lucky that her father is a stockbroker, who believes in starting a saving and investing program when a person is young. He helps her do the paperwork necessary to set up the IRA account, and to arrange for automatic contributions from her paycheck once a month. As an aside, for people who have this option available to them, the automatic withdrawals from a checking account can help implement the discipline necessary to make continuous contributions. She commences her IRA saving and investing plan at age twenty-five, and intends to continue to the plan until age sixty-five. She wants to be sufficiently disciplined so that she will make the monthly payment continuously, come rain or shine, and in tough times and easy times.

To summarize this example, she will contribute a little over $400 per month to total $5,000 per year, every month for the next forty years. She and her dad feel that it is realistic to try to earn an average compound rate of return of 6.5% over that forty-year period. Let's further assume that she starts the plan with zero dollars, but makes the monthly contribution steadily and continuously for the full forty years. If that is, in fact, the case, at the end of forty years, assuming the continuous compound rate of return of 6.5%, the total sum she will have at the end will be approximately $950,000. What an amazing result.

The point of these illustrations is to demonstrate the realistic power of this very basic tool, accessible by all who seek to save and invest. Suffice to say, it is extremely powerful when used patiently and consistently over time.

Many Wall Street professionals understand the power of compounding over time. But it is rare that they package their investments to take advantage of this powerful tool. The industry is geared to short-term gratification and short-term successes. (Remember, they get a fee for every transaction they make.) My hope, however, is that by presenting you with this tool, you are now in a better position to see if it is a tool that would work well for you.

POWERFUL TOOL #2: CONTINUOUS CONTRIBUTIONS AND DOLLAR COST AVERAGING

The investment tool of making continuous contributions to your saving and investing plan is powerful because it is one over which the saver has complete control. It is true that each of us has a limit over the dollar amounts we can afford to set aside for savings and investing. In fact, if we had no limits to our available dollars there would be no motive or reason for any of us to save and invest. However, within the reality of the limits to our available dollars, each of us has the freedom to decide how we allocate from the funds that are available. If we choose to use discipline and patience to build wealth for our future well-being, we have the right and the power to make those choices.

This tool or system of continuous contributions involves a couple of additional concepts, which, when combined with compounding over time, becomes an extremely powerful way to achieve success in reaching your financial goals. If you are aware of how these few concepts relate to each other, it will become clearer how powerful they can be.

One way to maximize the power of making a continuous contribution is to invoke the discipline of dollar cost averaging (DCA), on a systematic, continuous, and regular basis. When you decide to implement DCA, then the concept of the law of averages comes into play to smooth out the average rate of return of your investment program.

Within this tool, I will introduce DCA and the law of averages (convergence around the mean) to strengthen your understanding as to why I feel that continuous contributions to your savings and investing plan are so powerful. In fact, I'd almost go so far as to say that using this tool, when combined with the element of compounding over time, your investment plan cannot fail. If that's too bold of a statement, I clearly feel that, in most cases, it is true.

DCA is a style of investing that involves continually buying the same stock or the same mutual fund at regular periodic intervals over an extended period of time, usually several years. In most cases, a stock or mutual fund has a different price each time new money is used to purchase more shares. When you look back over time, there will be an average purchase price that you will have paid during the months or years of periodic purchases of that investment.

The reason this is such a powerful investment tool is that in the case of continuously buying the same stock or mutual fund over a long period of time, the price you pay for each share averages out in the long run. Even if stock prices are going up, the average price paid over time is usually lower than the highest price paid.

Of even greater importance is the element of continuously contributing to your saving and investing program. When you combine the tools of compounding over time and making continuous investment contributions, this has a far greater impact on the success of an investment program than the average rate of return one earns.

Let's compare an example of a one-time contribution versus one with continuous contributions. Two people each have a goal of building a nest egg of $1.0 million over a thirty- year period. Both people will grow their funds at the compound rate of 6% annually. The first person says she wants to invest a single lump sum at the beginning and let it accumulate for the thirty-year period. The second person plans differently and asks how much he can contribute monthly over the full thirty years to grow at the same expected rate of return.

To accumulate $1.0 million at a growth rate of 6% compounded annually over thirty years, the first person will have to contribute a lump sum of approximately $174,000 at the beginning. The second person, who wants to make continuous contributions, will have to contribute approximately $1,000 every month for thirty years, growing at the compound rate of 6%, to accumulate the sum of $1.0 million at the end.

Which approach seems less daunting to the average person: saving and investing $1,000 per month, or setting aside $174,000 at the beginning of the plan? If you are already rich, or have extensive borrowing power, the sum of $174,000 may not be daunting. For the rest of us, a plan involving habit and discipline to set aside $1,000 a month (no small task itself) appears more realistic.

The powerful tool of continuous contributions can give the average person who might have limited resources a realistic way of achieving their investment goals.

POWERFUL TOOL #3: HABIT, DISCIPLINE, AND CONSISTENCY

Here is a powerful investment tool, the main strength of which is the fact that its implementation is totally within the control of the investor. This tool involves conducting yourself more like a tortoise, who plods along steadily and on a straight line, and less like a rabbit, who jumps around back and forth, always distracted, and never able to make up its mind.

To understand discipline and consistency, you need to realize that seeking maximum rates of return, as Wall Street often stresses, has little to do with achieving investment success. Everyone emphasizes the importance of buying stocks at their lowest possible price and selling stocks at their highest possible price. The real world simply doesn't work that way for most of us. Nobody, I repeat, nobody can consistently buy stocks at the lowest low and sell at the highest high. The good news is that always buying low and selling high, is not required to be successful in achieving your financial goals. That's why the concept of DCA was introduced in the previous tool.

Of far greater importance than always striving to maximize your rate of return is implementing your disciplined and focused investment program. It is my opinion that you can achieve greater success by establishing your desired financial goal, similar to those we discuss in numerous examples throughout this book, and then staying the course with habit and discipline until your goal is achieved rather than constantly trying to beat the market and maximizing your return.

Let's take a step back for a moment and think of people who run small businesses. There are hundreds of thousands—perhaps millions—of American families who run all types of small businesses, not all of which are the high visibility McDonald's or Starbucks franchises. Many of them run local hardware stores, small restaurants, carpet cleaning services, or real estate offices. By and large, the majority of these business owners do not achieve record-breaking profits every year, but they are still successful and make a living for their families. Most of them are capable of achieving their realistic financial goals, as measured by their expectations. None of them operate their businesses with the expectation of maximizing profits. In other words, they don't act like failures if they don't set the world on fire with double-digits returns year after year. In most cases, they are satisfied if they can increase their revenues, year after year, at a rate that keeps up with the rate of inflation. So, my point is that we should use that same frame of mind when handling our savings and investing programs.

If we used the same discipline, consistency, and habitual contributions toward our saving and investing plans, as we do in running our small business, we would have more realistic expectations, and more realistic investment results. The fact that the stock market delivers annual returns that are sometimes extreme on either the upside or the downside doesn't mean that serious saver-investors should use those widely fluctuating variations as their primary goals. Investment goals should be expressed in terms of dollars, not percentage returns.

Employing discipline, habit, and consistency in your process of saving and investing will be far more reliable in moving toward your monetary goals than will those who feel the only measure of success is that of maximizing rates of return and beating the market.

Powerful Tool #4: Limited Diversification

Many experienced investors are familiar with the concepts of asset allocation and diversification of investments. This goes back to putting all of your eggs in the same basket. For example, many people with enough investment capital to diversify believe in putting some of their money in the stock market, some of their money in real estate, some of their money in bonds, and also keeping some of their money in cash.

This type of plan makes perfect sense, and nothing in this book is intended to contradict such sound thinking. The message in this section is to introduce the idea that, in some cases, investors or speculators overly diversify their investment categories, thereby defeating the purpose and effectiveness of diversification.

As a result, I am introducing the idea of "limited diversification" as being a substantially more powerful investment tool than a blind shotgun approach to diversifying for the sake of diversifying. As previously mentioned, many authors and researchers have studied the investment style of Warren Buffett, the world's wealthiest and most successful portfolio manager. Many years ago he established a system of limited diversification. During the early years of his success, some researchers might have felt that his investment method consisted of portfolio concentration—the opposite of portfolio diversification. The fact of the matter is that the size of his investment holding company, Berkshire Hathaway, became so large—something in the neighborhood of $100 billion in assets under management—that he had no choice but to diversify in the effort to be able to invest all his money. His corporate holding company owned entire companies in several instances, and he still had billions of dollars of cash to spend if he wanted to be fully invested.

Most of us average investors have the opposite problem. Individually speaking, we do not have enough cash to invest in all the different categories that we would like. But even with a limited amount of cash to invest, we can still learn a lesson from Buffett's style.

First, let's address the basic reason most sensible investors diversify, or spread around their investment dollars. Second, we will present a reason why limiting or tempering the idea of broad diversification will serve us as a powerful investment tool.

As already stated, nearly every individual with common sense realizes that it is a sound practice not to put all our eggs in one basket. Nobody has a crystal ball, so we do not know when certain types of investments will do well, and when that group will slow down and another category will do well. Allocating a percentage of our investment dollars into differing categories that do well at different times allows us the ability to enjoy the benefits of positive returns for a portion of our investments, even when other types are not so fortunate.

This level of common sense, logically speaking, only goes so far. Two observations support this critique. First, looking at the broader landscape, there are certain periods in our financial history where virtually all investments suffer. Certainly, the Great Depression of the 1930s is a clear instance. Likewise, there is ample evidence that almost all investment categories, such as real estate, stocks, bonds, commodities, even interest rates on cash deposits, have been excessively volatile from 2008 until the early of months of 2012. It is true that a few unique categories might have capitalized on the recent economic downturn, such as betting the farm on gold, or being a contrarian that "shorts" the market, but that is not the stuff of average investors saving for retirement.

Second, the opposite condition has a higher probability of occurring. There are periods when almost all investment categories go up steadily, no matter which category you place your investments. The period of the great bull market that ran from

1982 until 2001 (except for the brief recess of the crash of 1987) was a period where many investors were guilty of "confusing investment brilliance with a bull market." During that period, discussions of diversification and safe allocations were substituted with "dart throwing" at stock lists as a means for anyone to find a stock they expected to go up.

The final argument against blind, excessive diversification, for its own sake, is that it can unwind and undo all the fine work of many of the other powerful investment tools. If a person reads this book and learns the powerful lessons of what we can control in the world of investing, and what we cannot control, why destroy it all with excessive diversification? Finding a fundamentally sound investment takes a bit of work (although not by any means impossible). Blind diversification, "just to cover the bases," undoes that dedication and discipline. Furthermore, the facets of the economy that we cannot control, and that drag down or raise up all investments, like the ebbing tide, are not counteracted by diversification.

Let's not worry about things we cannot control, primarily because that stuff affects everyone, not just one or two of us unlucky ones. Instead, let's find out what limited diversification is, and wherein lies its special power, as employed by Buffett and other successful investors.

Asset allocation means choosing more than one class or category of investment, whose rise and fall are determined by differing economic variables. Simple examples are real estate versus stocks versus cash. Diversification means choosing more than one investment entity, whether it falls within the same or different investment class or category. Examples of diversification might be separate stock investments in Microsoft, ExxonMobil, Wal-Mart, and Kraft Foods.

Many people invest in mutual funds as a vehicle to achieve professional portfolio management, and to achieve diversification of their stock investments. A vast majority of mutual funds hold well in excess of 100 or more stock names. This investment style constitutes general diversification. The average person cannot hold a portfolio of several hundred different stock names because that usually requires several million dollars to be able to buy a meaningful amount of each stock name. For example, if a stock were trading at $50 per share, it would take $5,000 to purchase 100 shares. If you wanted a diversified portfolio of 150 names or more that would take an investment of at least $750,000. Virtually all mutual funds purchase substantially more than 100 shares of each stock name in their portfolios. They usually purchase several thousand shares of each name. At 1,000 shares per stock name, in a portfolio with 150 names, the investment amount becomes more like $7,500,000. Thus, full diversification becomes out of reach for most investors, unless they instead invest in the shares of their favorite mutual fund. Most mutual funds allow minimum investments starting at $1,000 or $2,500—a more realistic number for most investors.

As stated earlier, and more importantly, broad general diversification undoes all the good work of sound and powerful investment tools. With focused diversification, if one or two investments are underperforming, you can remove and replace them. Conversely, if you have a broad basket of stock names, there is greater potential for more bad fruit, and it is more difficult to identify and replace numerous stocks.

Would it not be more promising, or at least increase the probability of meeting your investment goals, to trim your portfolio to a limited selection of the best candidates—the players with the highest probability of success—and be in a better position to more closely observe and make substitutions as needed? Obviously, this is easier said than done and we will certainly be discussing how to do just that.

POWERFUL TOOL #5: LIMITED LEVERAGE

Many individual investors do not fully understand the concept of leverage. In its most common form, leverage means borrowing. If you are going to purchase a new home, you might desire to pay cash in the form of a 20% down payment, and then you borrow the remaining 80% from a bank, to use for paying the balance of the purchase price. In this instance, you would be using leverage at a ratio of 4 to 1. You're borrowing 80% and paying 20% in cash.

There are many benefits and many pitfalls in using leverage in any financial endeavor, whether it be buying a home, buying a car, buying stocks, buying a new business, or using a credit card to purchase the goods and services for everyday life. As a side note, using a debit card for making purchases is not leverage. Like writing a check, you need money in the account for it to be honored.

The most extensive use of leverage is by our US government. The government's borrowing is in the trillions of dollars. If any entity, whether it is a person, a corporation, or even the government, borrows so extensively that the amount it owes on its debt is larger than the assets it owns, it could eventually find itself insolvent, meaning bankrupt.

Similarly, the major pitfall of leverage is when borrowing becomes so extensive, without any repayment, that a company's or a person's amount of debt exceeds its assets. The major benefit of leverage is that you can purchase or invest in things using other people's money. The idea is to use a certain amount of leverage, thereby increasing the number of investments you can make, yet not getting so carried away so as to run the risk of your debt or borrowed money exceeding the value of your assets.

Limited leverage, as discussed here, means getting the benefits of leverage while avoiding the risks of its pitfalls. As just stated, if leverage allows one to make larger investments by using money borrowed from others, there is the potential for added profits or gains—certainly greater than one would earn without using leverage.

Before introducing an example, one additional point should be made. If you are going to use leverage at all, you should think, and act, like a "banker." What I mean by thinking like a banker is this: banks are in the business of borrowing and lending. That's how they make money. What most people don't realize is that when banks lend out money, they use borrowed funds to do so. The way banks make money at this endeavor is they use other people's money, which they borrow. In so doing, they have the ability to borrow at low-interest rates, and then they lend out the money at high-interest rates. In fact, in the world of banking, borrowing at low rates and lending at high rates is the same idea as "buying low and selling high" in the world of stock investing.

Now, as an example, suppose you have enough cash to purchase 1,000 shares of a stock selling at $50 per share. That would cost $50,000 (ignoring transactions costs for this illustration). Suppose that each share of stock pays $2 per share in dividends, annually. Finally, suppose after one year, you sell all your shares for $55 per share. What would be the total profit from owning the stock (again ignoring transaction costs and the effects of taxation)? Cash out of pocket was $50,000. Total profits were $7,000, based on receiving $2,000 in dividends during the year, plus receiving $5,000 from selling the stock at a $5 gain per share. Mathematically speaking, you enjoyed a 14% rate of return over the period of one year ($7,000 of profit from a $50,000 investment).

Let's add some "leverage." Please take my word for it that virtually all registered brokerage firms will allow investors to borrow money to make stock purchases. There are numerous strict rules for these types of transactions, which are called "buying stocks on margin." For this illustration, the general rule is that you can borrow an amount equal to the cash or stock "equity" you have in your account, as long as the money is used to buy stocks. So, if you wish to buy $100,000 worth of stock, you must have at least $50,000 cash in the account prior to the purchase. Again, the rules are strict and complex, but the practice is commonplace, so I am simplifying the explanation for the purpose of explaining the powerful tool of "limited leverage."

Continuing with the above illustration, suppose you are bullish, and feel confident the stock is going to rise in price during the coming year (although there is no way to be certain of this in the real world). In the case where you use leverage to purchase 1,500 shares instead of just 1,000 shares, you would acquire the additional shares by borrowing the extra amount needed, over and above the $50,000 available in cash. You would use leverage, and borrow $25,000 from the brokerage firm (in your margin account) to purchase an extra 500 shares (500 x $50 per share = $25,000). To make the illustration realistic, let us assume that the brokerage firm charges 6% interest annually on amounts borrowed from the firm.

Let's compare the results using leverage (borrowed funds) versus no leverage. Without leverage, as we computed above, the rate of return was 14% (based on receiving a profit of $7,000 on a $50,000 investment). What is the rate of return using leverage, borrowing in your margin account to purchase an additional 500 shares? The total gains of 1,500 shares bought at $50 per share and sold at $55 per share are $7,500. Earnings from dividends at the rate of $2 per share, for 1,500 shares, are $3,000. Total summary profits, before subtracting the cost of borrowing, equals $10,500 (= $7,500 + $3,000). Because you borrowed $25,000, the interest charges on that amount for one year is $1,500 (based on 6% of 25,000). The total profit in this case, having used leveraged borrowing to buy more shares, equals $9,000 = (1,500 x $5) + (1,500 x $2) − ($25,000 x .06).

Isn't that amazing? By using borrowing power (leverage) to increase the number of shares purchased, the dollar amount out of pocket remained the same, but the total return increased from $7,000 to $9,000, or from a 14% rate of return to an 18% rate of return.

The example just shown of course illustrated the best outcome. Using leverage comes with a number of risks, most of which depend on the price movement of the stock that is purchased. For example, if the stock instead of going up from $50 to $55 per share, goes down to $45 or even $40 per share, our investor would not just lose the $5,000 or $10,000, you would have lost by purchasing the original 1,000 shares. With the suggested leverage (borrowing $25,000 to purchase an additional 500 shares), if the stock dropped to $45 or even $40 per share, the loss would be $7,500 or even $15,000. Not a pretty picture.

Because of the downside risks, I feel that the use of excessive leverage (borrowing) is too risky. Adding leverage adds risk, along with the increased potential for profit. I believe in the power of sound stock investments, but I'm also a conservative investor. By using limited leverage, rather than maximum leverage, you increase the potential on the upside, and you limit the exposure to an adverse outcome that will cause financial setbacks or even financial ruin. Since there is a risk in every investment endeavor, an investor who chooses to use leverage for the potential of increasing upside profit should be careful and use only a controlled or limited amount of borrowing. The excess upside potential does not justify the excess risk.

Think about it. In the above scenario, the maximum leverage you could have used would have been to invest your $50,000 cash to buy 1,000 shares of stock, and then borrow the maximum of another $50,000 to buy a total of 2,000 shares of stock. If the stock increased from $50 per share to $55 or $60 or even $70 per share, you would have made double the amount you would have made without using leverage. But, the downside risk would have been more than any conservative investor should have to bear. If in this example, the stock would have gone down to $40 per share, the maximum leverage would have resulted in a loss of $20,000 on the investment, plus you would have to pay back the $50,000 borrowed, plus interest charges. If you are going to use leverage at all, limited leverage is the only sensible way to go.

Maximum leverage is crazy.

In summary, every corporation has a certain amount of debt. Those who control their debt are the healthy ones. They never worry about paying their bills. With limited leverage corporations increase the return on their invested capital, and individual investors can do the same.

POWERFUL TOOL #6: LIMITED HEDGING

What is hedging? People talk about hedging their bets. When you hedge, you make enough profit from the hedging activity to offset all or a portion of any loss if the bet or investment turns out poorly. What investors should know is that hedging is like buying insurance, and that always comes with a cost. Like insurance on your car or house, even if you never have an auto accident or house fire, you still pay insurance premiums every year so that you are protected if a catastrophe should occur when you might least expect it. That's hedging. Sometimes this is called spreading the risk of loss.

Not only does hedging come with a price, but it can also become extremely expensive, so much so that it could wipe out a good portion of your gain or profit. For example, suppose you own a stock for which you paid $25 per share four or five years ago. Now the stock price is $100 per share, and you don't want to sell it in case it goes even higher, and you do not want to be faced with a large capital gain tax. You still might want to protect the gains you have earned in the event the stock price drops. How could one hedge this investment to lock in your gains to this point?

An investor in such a situation could purchase what is called a "put option." This type of hedging vehicle would protect your stock price in the event it should fall below a certain price level the investor selects. A put option resembles an insurance policy in many respects. Like insurance policies, you have to pay a premium every time you buy a put option that is an option to protect your stock price in the event it goes down. And, like an insurance policy, the put option is only good for a certain period of time. To continue with the protection, you would have to pay premiums for another period of time.

For example, if you want to protect your $100 stock from going down below $95 per share, it might cost you $2 per share every six months to protect that stock from going down below $95. What a put option does, in this example, is to allow you to sell each of your shares for $95 on a stock exchange during the next six-month life of the put option. If the stock price stays above $95 per share, you would not need to take advantage of the put option, because you would only get $95 per share if you "exercise" the put option you bought. You would just hold on to the stock, because it is worth more than $95, the amount protected with the purchase of the "put." Only if the stock price fell below $95 per share would you exercise the put, meaning you would use the services of the stock exchange to force another person to pay $95 per share for the stock. Note that the right to force someone else to pay $95 per share would expire after six months.

If you wish to continue with protecting (meaning hedging) the stock price, you would have to pay a new premium for the next six months, and the cost of the new premium will depend on market conditions at that time. It could be more than $2 per share or less than $2 per share when the new put option is purchased.

The above example is presented for illustrative and explanatory purposes only, and is not intended as a statement of the actual price of a put option on any particular stock. The actual cost of buying a put option varies dramatically, depending on the price of the stock it relates to, and several other factors that are beyond the scope of this book.

As stated earlier, buying a put option is just one form of hedging against losses and can be expensive over time, such that it could eventually wipe out all the power of your successful investment. One might call the purchase of a put option a complete hedge against downside losses. But you need to decide on an individualized basis whether or not it wipes out a reasonable opportunity for profit and decide whether it is worth the cost.

There is no such thing as a perfect hedge against downside risk. This is because there is no such thing as an absolute guarantee against loss, or absolute certainty that you can earn a guaranteed rate of return. It is my belief that a better approach toward protecting your investments against downside losses would be to take steps toward limited or partial downside protection, while allowing for the higher probability of upside gains. In other words, just like dealing with insurance on your car or home, most of us accept a "deductible" amount that we are willing to pay out of pocket in the event of damage or loss of property. The same concept should be applied to your investments. In this manner, you can somewhat soften the blow when the economy goes south while still leaving yourself in a position to profit if economic conditions are favorable.

I'm not an expert on hedging, and I don't ever care to be. Some say there is no such thing as a perfect hedge. One cannot bet on both red and black at the roulette wheel and still make a profit. But to me, hedging is not a matter of betting on red and black and trying to win on both. If we are going to use that analogy, it is a matter of betting on red to win and betting on black to break even or only lose a little. And there is a huge difference. In the stock market, there is a system of selling stocks "short," which basically allows stock traders to profit if stock prices go down. Studies and performance reporting by portfolio managers who specialize in "shorting" stocks on a consistent basis show that they do no better over the long run than typical investors who buy stocks hoping to profit from upside markets. There are certainly exceptions to every generalization, but constantly betting against the tide is not a perfect hedge.

So why is "limited hedging" a powerful investment tool and how can an investor employ this technique? Limited hedging says that a person is willing to give up a small amount of upside profit to protect against excessive losses. Buying low-cost insurance that includes paying a high deductible in the event you have to make a claim of loss might properly be called a limited hedge. How can an investor do this in the stock market, or in other financial investments?

In reality, the purchase of put options to a small degree might be a good trade-off against big losses, but not so costly as to wipe out all of your potential profits. Another technique often used by sophisticated stock traders is called "stop-loss" trading orders. An investor who owns stocks in a brokerage account can instruct their broker to enter a stop-loss order on their stocks. This stop-loss order says to the stock exchange that if your stock falls to a certain price point, there is a standing order to sell the stock at that price, or the best price available once the stock hits the selected price. Using our previous example, if you owned a stock currently worth $100 per share and wanted to ride it out to see if it would continue to go up, but were worried that it would go down, you could put a stop-loss order in for the stock at $95. Such downside protection techniques are somewhat complex, carrying with them pitfalls for the inexperienced stock trader, and are not recommended for implementation without a detailed explanation from an investment advisor or member of a reputable brokerage firm.

The concept of limited hedging includes not just protecting on the downside, but includes the potential of enjoying benefits on the upside as well. One example of protecting on the downside while also participating on the upside is a technique of buying stocks and selling "covered calls" on those same stocks. This technique constitutes limited hedging because it does not prevent complete loss of your investment, but it does reduce the amount of potential loss if a stock loses value. Meanwhile, if a stock increases in price, this technique allows for enjoying a certain amount of upside potential. The price an investor pays for engaging in selling covered calls is to cut off unlimited gains on the upside. During volatile and choppy stock market conditions, using trading techniques such as covered calls may be a good way to engage in limited hedging.

POWERFUL TOOL #7: LOW FEES, LOW COMMISSIONS, AND LOW TAXES

As you know by now, one of the themes of this book is urging investors to know what you can and cannot control. You cannot control the state of the economy, the rates of inflation and interest rates, the costs of housing, the price of gasoline or food, and you cannot control the prices of stocks you buy. But you can attempt to control the amount of fees you pay for professional advice, the commissions you pay to trade stocks, and with the help of seasoned taxation specialist, you can control the taxation rate that you pay on your investments.

Maybe this powerful investment tool should be called "Knowing what you can control and what you cannot control." Individuals can control, to a large degree, the amount of fees and commissions you pay, and how often you trigger taxable events. Perhaps it would be naïve to suggest that an investor could completely control the amount of fees, commissions, and taxes they pay. It might be more realistic to say that an investor can strongly influence the amount or rate they pay in the form of fees, commissions, and taxes.

For any reader who is not familiar with the commissions and fees charged by brokerage firms and investment advisory firms, such items are fully disclosed when you open an investment account with such firms. A detailed discussion of commissions, fees, and taxation rates on different types of investments is beyond the scope of this book. Any taxation professional will be pleased and motivated to explain such concepts to anyone who asks.

A few brief comments on these topics will at least put us on the same page when discussing this tool. Commissions are the money charged by stock brokerage firms for transacting stock trades for their clients. Prior to the emergence of discount brokerage firms, such as Schwab and Fidelity, trading commissions were very high. Commissions were charged to clients at high rates, both when they purchased shares, and when they sold shares. Eventually, by the 1970s, the discount brokerages emerged; and later, by the late 1990s, the online brokerage services emerged, whereby commissions for stock trades decreased significantly. Thus, it should not be looked at as "you get what you pay for" when it comes to commissions and fees. Be smart and shop around. It is safe to say, the lower an investor keeps their payment of commissions, fees, and taxes, the higher their return on their investment will be, all other factors being equal.

The approach to taxes is fairly straightforward. Here are two examples, one pretty much self-evident, and the other rather surprising. In the first example, we will compare two similar investments, both yielding an average compounded rate of return of 10% annually, and where one investment is taxed at a lower rate than the other. In the second example, we will compare two similar investments, both yielding an average compounded rate of return of 10% annually. With one investor, the annual earnings will be taxed every year, and with the other investor, there will be a deferral of the taxation until many years later. The tax rate will be the same for both investors, but with a deferral of taxation for one investor, the results might surprise you.

Starting with the first example, there are two investors, each with $10,000 to invest, and each will enjoy a 10% annual compounded rate of return, and each will leave the money invested for twenty years. The first investor will have their investment taxed at the rate of 25% taxation at the end of every year for twenty years. The second investor will have their investment taxed at the rate of only 20% taxation at the end of every year for twenty years.

The difference in the outcome of the two investments, after

taxes are paid at differing rates, should be self-evident. The first investor, who will be taxed at a rate of 25%, will have a resulting sum of $42,478.51 after all taxes have been paid at the end of twenty years. The second investor, who will be taxed at a lower rate of 20%, will have a resulting sum of $46,609.57 after all taxes have been paid at the end of twenty years. It's clear that the investor who has a lower tax rate will have a higher after-tax return, and more dollars to spend, then the person with the higher tax rate. The person with the higher tax rate would have to obtain a higher rate of return to obtain the same after-tax dollar amount as the person with a lower tax rate.

Now let's look at the second example. Again, there are two investors, each with $10,000 to invest, and each will enjoy a 10% annual compound rate of return, and each will have their money invested for twenty years. Each investor will have earnings from the investment taxed at the rate of 25%.

In this example, the first investor has his earnings on his $10,000 investment taxed every year, at the tax rate of 25%. At the end of twenty years, with the appropriate taxes paid each year along the way, the investor will have the resulting sum of $42,478.51 after all taxes have been paid. The second investor, who also invests $10,000, has the taxes on the earnings of her investment deferred until the end of the twenty years. Let's assume her investment was held in an IRA account or another type of qualified retirement plan. At the end of twenty years, the total sum resulting from the investment will be $67,275.00, but will now have to be reduced by the 25% tax rate that needs to be paid. After payment of the taxes at the end of twenty years, the investor will have the resulting sum of $50,456.25. Even after paying taxes, the second investor ends up with more dollars by deferring taxes until the end of the investment period.

The amazing thing is that both investors in this second example are taxed at the same rate of 25%, yet one has more dollars in the end than does the other. The powerful investment tool of lower taxes, and in this case deferred taxes, gives an improved result. This improved result has nothing to do with Wall Street, the state of the economy, or the ups and downs of the stock market. This powerful investment tool is available to almost everyone who cares to use it.

The point of this tool is quite simple and clear. In the case of payment of fees, commissions, and even taxation rates, you, the investor, have a certain amount of control. To the extent that you are able, it behooves you to take advantage of the ability to control your costs of investing. If you can lower any or all of them, you will increase your compound rate of return accordingly.

POWERFUL TOOL #8: INVESTING IN COMPANIES WITH STRONG FINANCIAL STATEMENTS

It is clear to me that people who have been investing for many years tend to have their own opinions on what type of investments make them feel comfortable. Some people only know real estate, others like investing in gold or precious gems, and other people are more comfortable investing in conservative bonds and fixed income securities. In recent years, a good percentage of investors have even been drawn toward annuities and life insurance as their investment vehicles of preference. Most people know that over the years, stocks and mutual funds have served as stable sources of long-term investing, especially as a source for funding retirement plans such as IRA accounts and 401(k) plans. Depending on economic conditions, especially during periods of downward stock prices, many investors shy away from stock investments altogether. They don't like seeing their stock prices fluctuate up and down like a roller coaster. In a rough economic environment, they may view stocks as too risky for their psyche.

I want to make a case for committing to investing in high-quality stocks, and sticking to that program through thick and thin, during good times and bad. The reasons behind this recommendation are so numerous I probably cannot list them all, but I will try to highlight some of the more convincing reasons. Most importantly, it is my position that the stock of a company with strong financial statements is a powerful investment tool.

To begin with, I should define what I mean by companies with strong financial statements. Most investors may not even understand the complex financial statements of large public corporations. However, there are some basic elements to a company's strong financial condition that most investors should be able to understand. I will focus on just a few key variables that should provide evidence of any company's financial condition, as to whether it is strong or not. All the information I'll be referring to is available on most online search engine providers, without charge, such as Yahoo, Google, MSN, Bloomberg, CNBC, and many others.

The key metrics I tend to look for are rising revenues and rising earnings in recent years. In addition, I look for a ratio of low debt in comparison to the net equity of the company. Equally important is evidence of a steady dividend paid to shareholders over the years, and even better if there is a track record of periodically increasing the amount of the dividend.

The overwhelming importance of the power of this investment tool is that when you invest in a company with these key metrics, you know your investment is keeping up with inflation. If such a company continually increases its earnings, and the amount of dividend you receive is continuing to increase, you know your investment is not being devalued by the impact of inflation. That alone makes this a powerful investment tool. The fact that we also look for companies with relatively low debt, especially those that have a consistent dividend payment schedule, adds to our confidence that the dividend payments will continue. We even feel justified in expecting that the dividends will increase over time. These metrics are usually good evidence of the stability of such companies, both as to their stock prices and their viability.

I have labeled this powerful tool as investing in companies with strong financial statements. Another way of looking at this approach would be to call it investing in "value" companies. However, labeling it in that fashion would run the risk of it being confused with what Wall Street often refers to as investing in "value" stocks. As I pointed out in the previous section dealing with Wall Street misconceptions, Wall Street often refers to investors looking for value stocks as those looking for stocks on the cheap, meaning bottom fishing for low-priced stocks. That's not what we're talking about here.

If an investor is searching for stocks that are priced below their current fair value, as estimated by a consensus of Wall Street stock analysts, it should not be made to appear that using such criteria means searching for low-priced stocks. Just because a stock is priced low does not mean it is a good value, and just because a stock is priced high doesn't mean it's a bad value. Many excellent stocks that meet the criteria I have presented above are priced well above $100 per share. The stock of any company with a track record of rising revenues, rising earnings, low debt, and rising dividends has the potential of being a powerful investment tool. If such a stock is a powerful investment tool, it is a good value.

Let's be clear about one thing: investing in consistently solid financial statements is not a formula for picking stocks that are going to be high flyers and hit super home runs with your money. That type of stock picking works out for only a select few who are lucky gamblers. And if you feel compelled to search for the next stock market super winner, then I sincerely wish you good luck!

My main purpose with this book is to introduce common sense concepts for building a financial nest egg for your future financial goals. The tools I am presenting are accessible to anyone who wants to use them. Investing in the stock of companies that have the type of sound financial statements I've described in this chapter is totally within your control. If you employ the criteria I have set out here, or even develop your criteria for what you consider to be strong companies, you can control the decision of whether or not to invest in such companies. In fact, we have finally touched upon one of the true beauties of Wall Street: Wall Street is the only place that gives all of us access to this type of powerful investment tool. Every one of us can decide how much or how little (within our means) to invest in one or more of these financially strong companies.

POWERFUL TOOL #9: TREATING INVESTING LIKE RUNNING A BUSINESS

Whether you are a business owner, work for a company, work for yourself, or run a household, you inherently understand the concepts of how to run a business. The tool of approaching investing like running a business is simply a matter of being objective, and making sound economic decisions. Here are some basic ideas that are intended to make investing much more rewarding, satisfying, and less stressful than distractions from Wall Street present. Eliminate emotion. Be objective. Generate cash flows. Think like a banker. Operate your stock portfolio as if it the stocks were your business inventory. If you want a different mental picture to think about, think of your stocks in a similar way you would handle a piece of investment real estate. It's true that there are distinct differences between stock investing and dealing with inventory in a small business, or investing in income-producing real estate. The important similarity we're talking about here is your frame of mind, meaning your attitude and mental approach to stock investing. In that regard, there is no reason why investing in stocks shouldn't be done from the same mindset as running a small business or managing income-producing real estate property.

Think about it. Suppose you own a small five-unit apartment complex that you rent out to tenants. Do you appraise the value of your real estate ten or twenty times a day? Or if you manage a shoe store, or a neighborhood convenience store, or a fast food franchise, do you constantly run around checking the price tags of your entire inventory throughout the day, every day? If you don't constantly worry about the price of your business inventory or the daily changes in the value of your rental property, why are we programmed by Wall Street to continually worry about the daily changes in our stock prices? Believe me, we all do it— and I candidly include myself.

Wall Street technology and the popular media give us the tools to see stock quotes and price changes every microsecond during market trading hours. We don't have that technology imposed on our business inventory and real estate holdings. Actually, we do have the technology, but the reality is that business inventory and real property do not trade with the extreme speed and frequency that securities do. As a result, prices in those sectors are substantially more stable. While I admit that I frequently check my stock prices, the difference is that I do not allow myself to be unreasonably reactionary.

This brings me to my second point about treating investing like a running a small business. Be proactive, not reactive. If you own a rental property and there is high rental demand in your area coupled with an availability shortage, it would probably make sense to reasonably raise your rent. But you certainly shouldn't reduce the rental price because a house three blocks away had cockroach issues. Likewise, if you own a local food mart and the National Dental Association posts an article on the Huffington Post condemning the act of chewing gum, are you going to immediately drop the price of all the gum in your store to a penny? Obviously, the answer is no. You are not going to overreact. Then, under the same concept, you should stay the course with your investments and allow the natural course of time, compounding, hedging, selectivity, and other powerful tools to run their course.

If investors establish a frame of mind that their goals should be to achieve a realistic rate of return, on average, over an extended period of time, then short-term price swings should be ignored. Suggestion: I encourage investors to take a "big picture" approach, even if Wall Street and the media make us believe that the sky is going to fall as a result of second-by-second price changes of our stocks. Remember, constant buying and selling makes Wall Street money, not you.

Let's take another perspective, and this one might help convince you to be an investor, not a speculator. Why is it that people who own income-producing real estate are generally not concerned about changes in prices or values of their holdings? There are two reasons I can think of. Firstly, their focus is on the rental income, on the vacancy factor, and meeting all their expenses without any deficits. It sounds just like a business. They are concerned with the cash flow, the rents, and any vacancies that will interrupt the flow of cash. Secondly, their properties are not for sale every second of every day. The only time that the prices going up and down make a difference to a property owner is when an investor is either buying or selling. If you own stocks, is your portfolio constantly for sale, or do you plan to hold it for an extended period of time? If you plan to hold stocks that you think are of high quality for two, three, or four years or more, then constantly checking their stock prices is a surefire way to the asylum. It can indeed drive us nuts. Many brokerage firms send their account holdings a monthly statement. Maybe that's a good rule of thumb. A wise investor always keeps track of what is going on with their money, yes indeed. If you're not an active stock trader, and are holding investments for the long term, checking the stock prices in your portfolio once a month is probably a good compromise. I assure you, you are not going to lose control of your investments if you keep yourself informed on a once-a-month basis. There's a good chance your stress level will drop dramatically.

There might be one major exception to only checking your stock prices once a month. If you are in the market to either buy more stock to add to your existing portfolio, or you have reasons to sell some of your holdings, then, of course, you need to bring yourself current on the prices of stocks you plan to buy or sell.

The thrust of this section is that treating one's stock portfolio like a business will allow you to make sound, proactive, unemotional decisions. In summary, approaching stock investing with a frame of mind similar to running a small business or income-producing real estate investing is something an investor can control. Being objective, being conservative in one's business decisions, and taking steps to reduce the emotional stress can serve as a truly powerful tool in building your desired nest egg or body of wealth.

POWERFUL TOOL #10: KNOWING WHAT YOU CAN AND CANNOT CONTROL

We've mentioned several times that there are numerous investment types from which to choose, any of which have the potential to generate compound rates of return over a long period of time. I will discuss these in greater detail in Section 4. In many respects, this tenth tool reiterates the power of investing in companies with strong financial statements. If you are beginning to understand the philosophy of this book, you might agree with me that the stock of strong companies should be a core and natural component of every investor's arsenal. It seems obvious, right? But if we agree it's so obvious, why don't most people adhere to it?

Let us return for a moment to a few of the misconceptions presented earlier in this book. Are you an investor or a speculator? Did you beat the index last year? The only good market is an up market. There's a crisis in Europe. What's going to happen if so-and-so gets elected?

Each of these expressions is a distraction to sound investing, brought on by the media and marketing from Wall Street. As I pointed out in the section about treating investing like a business, if you're a small business owner, do you change how you run your business when the market plunges five hundred points, or an earthquake occurs in Asia, or oil prices spike up because of a political revolt in the Mideast? Yes, we are aware and often worry when these unstable events occur, but what we do every day in running our businesses, and even running our households does not change dramatically on a day-to-day basis. News on Fox, CNN, or CNBC does not usually change our daily routine or our expectations from our family, friends, or even our job descriptions.

Another point I made earlier in the book relates to one of my distinctions between investing and speculating. With most types of speculation, such as the lottery, picking the winning horse, or finding the newest hot stock, only a few can be winners—generally, only a lucky few. Their success is usually at the expense of all the other people who play the game. With true investing, everyone who participates has the potential (although not a guarantee) of being successful.

There is plenty of room for everyone who chooses to do so, to use the powerful tools of investing and to be successful at it.

This tool of making core investments and of knowing what you can and cannot control is just such a tool. And we can all use it.

The more we understand and realize that none of us general members of the public can control the state of the economy, or the ups and downs of the stock market, or the financial crisis in Europe, or the price of gasoline at the pump, or even which political party controls Congress and the White House, the more we should be able to avoid the distractions that create the most stress.

By way of contrast, there are many things we individually can control in relation to our savings and investing plan. It is my belief that the items you can control have a more direct impact on the success or failure of your investment plan than the things you cannot control. Unfortunately, far too many people expend way too much energy on the items they cannot control instead of those that they can.

Let's list four items we should all be able to control, each of which I feel has a dramatic impact on the potential success of your savings and investing program. First, you can control your selection of investment goals and the investment and savings plan that you implement. Second, you can control the category of investments that you select as your vehicle for implementing your investment plan. Third, you can control whom you select to be part of your investment team, which we might to refer to as your "team." These are people who will provide the valuable input and expertise to help you fill in the blanks where you might lack the full knowledge to make reasonable and rational decisions. In fact, you can control whether you want a team at all. If you want to do it all on your own, regarding your savings and investing activities, you are in control of that decision. Fourth, you definitely can control which of the powerful tools of investment that you choose to use for implementing your savings and investing plan.

With these basic parameters that any saver-investor can control, it becomes paramount that one who seeks to achieve his or her investment goals should have core investments with which to implement an investment plan. By core investments, I do not mean that I am going to urge anyone to stray from their comfort level in selecting key investments with which to grow their nest egg. Any particular investment or category of investments with which I am most comfortable may not be the same as that of any of my readers. The beauty of the world of economics, and Wall Street, in particular, is that there are numerous choices from which any of us can choose to serve as our group of core investments.

By core investing, I am referring to a category of investments such as stocks, or bonds, or mutual funds, or real estate, or variable annuities, or precious gems, or whatever category of investing that meets the comfort level of the investor. It is strongly recommended that an investor select a basic category that meets their comfort level, and that should serve as the core for accomplishing their financial savings goal.

There are numerous investment categories, in addition to your core category, in which you can make investments. It is recommended when implementing your savings and investment plan that these additional categories be reserved for side investments made from money other than that designated for growing your nest egg. It is not recommended that you complicate your investment and savings plan by going astray from the core investments. The core investments, the ones that you designate as such, have the greater probability than do the side investments of achieving the long-term average compounded rate of return necessary to achieve your investment goals, and to build your financial nest egg.

We again return to the concept of knowing what you can and cannot control in the endeavor to build your financial nest egg. It is true that no individual can control the ups and downs of the stock market, or the general economy, but the selection and maintenance of your core investments are something you can control.

If you have the resources and the expertise to manage income-producing real estate, for example, then you should stick to those types of core investments. That's what you know, and that's what you're familiar with. It makes more sense to have an investment discipline with that style of investing than it does to engage in commodity investing, or stock investing, or even bond investing, which could create stress and anxiety for you.

There are no guarantees in any investment category, but engaging in investments that you are familiar with certainly enhances your opportunity to generate the average annual rates of return that you seek to reach your target financial goals successfully.

It is also appropriate to again mention that the formation of your investment "team" is something that you, as a saver and investor, can control. Whether you invest on your own, or you employ the service of an investment professional, or just team up with a family member, you control whom you choose to be on your team. You might have to expend some energy to find the right professional to assist you in planning and implementing your goals. You are the one who decides who will be on your team. If the people on your team aren't compatible, or aren't serving your needs, you have the power to replace them.

In summary, knowing what you can and cannot control, and adhering to your selected core investments, in addition to putting together the right team through whom you will execute your personalized plan, constitutes the final powerful tool in our list.

A few concluding comments for this section. I have presented what I believe are ten powerful investment tools with the intent to assist savers and investors in achieving their investment goals. This is not to say there aren't other powerful tools. Some of you might say there are eleven or twelve powerful tools you can think of. Others might say that the tools I've presented in this section are not all so powerful, and that there are only eight—or at the most, nine—powerful tools.

I don't have a problem with that, because the idea of presenting these tools is to make readers think about what really controls and impacts the growth of their investment nest egg. You should have noticed that none of these tools includes predicting the direction of the stock market or beating the Dow Jones Industrial Average.

Not all of these tools need to be implemented for you to achieve your investment goals. You can use them all, or just a few, and still achieve investment success. Individuals are each different, and some of these tools will appeal to some investors more than others. The common denominator for all of these tools is that they do not require magic or perfect timing to assist investors in reaching their financial goals. In the next section, we are now ready to develop your financial plan.

To assure readers that this book is not a disguised attempt to remove or replace Wall Street with some other type of institution, or to assign blame to anyone other than a collective of us all, I have tried to encourage readers to employ these powerful tools of investing by one means or another. It's excellent if you can gain access to them through your Wall Street representative. Alternatively, you might be an investor who works individually. Even if you access these tools through other means, I still urge you to use as few or as many of them as you deem necessary to help achieve your financial goals.

The tools discussed in this section are by no means the only investment tools available to an investor, but this group of ten were presented for their simplicity of understanding and ease of availability by virtually all who invest in stocks and other mainstream Wall Street investments, e.g., bonds, mutual funds, annuities, etc.

A brief review of the ten powerful tools is as follows:

Tool #1: Compounding Over Time

Tool #2: Continuous Contributions and the Law of Averages

Tool #3: Habit, Discipline, and Consistency

Tool #4: Limited Diversification

Tool #5:Limited Leverage

Tool #6: Limited Hedging

Tool #7:Low Fees, Low Commissions, and Low
Taxes

Tool #8:Investing in Companies with Strong
Financial Statements

Tool #9: Treating Investing Like Running a
Business

Tool #10: Knowing What You Can and Cannot
Control

Tools #1 & #2: The tools of compounding over time and continuous contributions go hand in hand. If a person invests $100 and lets it compound at even a modest annual rate for thirty or forty years, the growth of that investment will be substantial. Additionally, if we add to the original $100 a continuous contribution of another $100 every year for thirty or forty years, the amount of growth is remarkable. Who would imagine that a mere $100 per year could turn into $8,000 or $9,000 after thirty-plus years?

If you could sock away $100 each every month for thirty years and earn a 6% annualized rate of return on that saved money, you would accumulate more than $100,000 by the end of a thirty-year period. And if you earn a relatively high income, and have the discipline to set aside tenfold that number each month, you would be on pace to accumulate more than $1.0 million in thirty-plus years.

The powerful tools of compounding and continuous contributions are available to us all, at whatever level we can afford.

Tool #3: The tool of habit and discipline seems so self-evident that one wonders why it is listed separately as a powerful tool. The reason is that so many individual investors operate without discipline and consistency that we feel by emphasizing the power and benefits of such conduct perhaps more people would employ these basic concepts. Being disciplined and habitual will allow compounding and continuous contributions to do their work.

Tools #4, #5, & #6: These three tools of limited diversification, limited leverage, and limited hedging, if used excessively and not in a limited or controlled way, might expose an investor to a level of risk that could easily wipe out your entire investment resources. We would never advocate that. By suggesting that investors use limited diversification, limited leverage, and limited hedging, we hope that investors will keep the potential for serious risk of loss in check.

Limited diversification means not putting all your eggs in one basket of investments, and also avoiding an excessive number of baskets, so that when one does well, it helps the overall program.

Limited leverage means that a controlled amount of borrowing can give an investor more bang for the buck; but excessive borrowing, whether in a brokerage margin account or from other sources, exposes an investor to the risk of huge losses when things go sour. If an investor refrains from borrowing more than they can afford to lose, a downturn in an investment or the economy, in general, will not wipe out their entire investment portfolio.

Limited hedging means that excessive downside protection can work against upside potential. There is a dollar cost to hedging, not unlike buying an insurance policy. If the cost of insurance is too high, it can offset all the profits and gains from the initial investment.

Tool #7: Low fees, low brokerage commissions, and low taxes can help keep annual investment returns from being reduced excessively. If an investment produces a 7% annual return, but the impact of fees, commissions, and taxes equals 2%, the net effect is a 5% annual return. If a person invested $10,000 and enjoyed a steady 7% annual return for the next ten years, they would end up with approximately

$20,000 by the end of that period, absent any reduction by fees, commissions, and taxes. If fees and commissions lowered the returns to 5% annually, the growth would end up being approximately $16,000 by the end of the ten years. Assuming taxation at the rate of 20%, the total amount on hand at the end of ten years would be approximately $13,000. As you can see, the impact of fees, commissions, and taxation reduced the final buildup of the investment by approximately 70%.

Even a small reduction in the fees and costs of investing can improve the amount an investor can take to the bank.

Tool #8: This tool requires some homework on the part of the investor. Investing in the stocks of companies with strong financial statements generally, involves stocks which hold up better than most even in down markets. Information about the balance sheets, income statements, and cash flow statements is available on numerous publicly available websites, such as Google, Yahoo, Bloomberg, CNBC, MSN, Fidelity, Schwab, TD Ameritrade, Morningstar, and others.

Strong financial statements usually involve firms with low debt, growth in earnings, and dividends that are steady and usually increasing over the long term. The stock of firms that show steady financial strength, when other parts of the economy are shaky, usually hold up better than most.

Tools #9: This is closely related to Tool #8. If you are treating your investments as if you are running a business, it means you are objective and unemotional about your investments. Cash flow is important in the running of a business, so is picking stocks that pay dividends and generate cash flow consistent with that type of thinking.

Likewise, is researching to find stocks of companies with strong financial statements, and especially those that pay dividends, consistent with treating your stock investments like running a business.

When you run a business, you are trying to be disciplined, consistent, and objective regarding the products you sell, the prices you charge, and the expenses you incur. Stock investing should be handled similarly.

Tool # 10: Knowing what you can and cannot control does not appear, on the surface, to have much impact on your investing. I have a different view about that. There are two facets of this tool that could make a difference in how you handle your investments and how you feel about the process. You cannot control changes in the economy, changes in market conditions, or changes in stock prices. On the other hand, you can control which stock investments you choose, and the amount of money you place in the investments of your choice. Some of these choices are indeed limited by your level of wealth, but from that limiting amount, you alone decide what percentage you will invest in any one security.

There are at least two critical lessons to be learned from this powerful tool. First, as an investor, you should expend most of your energies on items over which you have control, and not on events over which you have no control. If your research is thorough, you have control over the selections you make of stocks or other investment instruments. That is a far better place to expend your energy and resources than spending time worrying about the general economy, or events in foreign countries, or other things that you cannot control.

The second lesson emanating from this powerful tool is that you should try your utmost not to lose sleep or develop stress over bad news reported by the media about the general economy. I am not suggesting that bad news is not bad news, but that there is nothing you can do about it. You should not stress out or lose sleep over such things, because they are not personal to you. If bad news impacts you directly, I assure you, it impacts everyone.

I feel this is especially true with respect to your investments in stocks or other Wall Street investments. You can control the types of securities you invest in. If your research does not produce investment selections that meet with your satisfaction, you can control whether or not you put your money into such investments.

By way of summary of this section of the book, if you concentrate on maximizing energies and the application of your resources on the segment of Wall Street investing that you can control, and not get distracted by news about areas you cannot control, you will have less stress and better investment results.

SECTION 3:

YOUR FINANCIAL PLAN

Establishing & Understanding Your Financial Goals

Even if we don't think about it a great deal, most of us have financial goals that fall into one of two categories. For one, planning for retirement is our major concern, so that is the first category. It's not because we look forward to getting old, but we contemplate the need for financial security after a point in time when we will no longer have the same revenue stream we have during our working years. For our purposes, let's think of retirement as the point in your life when you stop earning revenue from your primary career or profession, and your income comes from sources other than your labor or professional efforts. The most common sources of income during retirement are from Social Security, distributions from retirement plans, and from investments.

Our second category of financial goals pretty much includes everything else for which a person or family would want to save and invest. These items might include things like saving up for a cruise around the world, a shuttle ride into outer space, a wedding for your child, a down payment on a house, a college fund for grandchildren, a new car, or even just an emergency fund. It is simply those things beyond our daily cost of living.

Most of the discussions in this section will focus on saving and investing for a secure retirement. In addition, I will present some examples of saving and investing to accumulate money for the other goals as well. It is my hope and intent that you will discover that the process of saving and investing for any financial goal is pretty much the same. You learn how to identify and categorize your financial goals. Then you develop a personalized process of saving and investing based on your goals and means. Then you simply execute your plan and make sensible adjustments along the way.

The Savings and Investing Process

I feel this book is unique in that the process of saving your money to be able to fulfill your financial dreams, and the process of investing the money you have saved, both go hand in hand. I firmly believe you cannot do one successfully unless you also do the other.

Most people who are serious and determined to build a financial nest egg usually think in terms of putting away money for safekeeping. They think of saving for the future as requiring discipline and sacrifice. When they save for the long term, they feel they are giving up something in the short term that would provide them with immediate gratification. Saving for the future is often viewed as a painful chore.

My premise in this section of the book is that accumulation of a financial nest egg or major goals, for whatever reason, includes more than just the disciplined process of saving and socking away your cash. If you seek to build a nest egg for the future, no matter the purpose or the goal, the steps that increase the probability of success require implementation of two key elements. The action step of saving, while essential to be successful, is only half the process. The companion activity, equally essential, is that of investing the money you have been saving.

In the previous section of the book, we discussed ten powerful investment tools available to all of us who wish to use them. One of those tools is discipline. Discipline is what is required to be a successful saver. Another of those tools is continuous contribution. This is the tool that takes savings and submits it to the investment process. Both of these tools are completely within the control of the individual involved. It is true that the dollar amounts will vary, depending on what is available in each individual's situation, but it is equally true that these tools are essential cornerstones to accomplishing your financial goals.

Some of the more conservative thinkers may feel that saving alone is the best approach because investing introduces the risk of loss to the process—especially in a volatile economy. My response to this would be simple. For most of us, saving without a plan to make the money we set aside grow will greatly reduce our ability to accumulate enough money to meet our financial goals. The simple truth is that most of us do not earn enough disposable income to amass the nest egg necessary to accomplish our short- or long-term goals without introducing some method of making that money grow. A mattress can burn, a cookie jar can be stolen, and the money sitting in a safety deposit box loses its buying power at the rate of inflation.

Alternatively, for the more aggressive risk takers out there, the volume and frequency with which you save your money are irrelevant if your investment strategy is one of pure speculation because you can lose it faster than you make it. Thus, the heart of this section is predicated on a sound balance between saving with regularity and continuous (responsible) contributions.

If we understand that saved dollars can work for us in ways that our jobs and careers and physical labor cannot, then we improve substantially the probability of reaching whatever financial goals we set. If we understand that the purpose of this book is to offer methods by which we can make sound investments by using the tools afforded to us wisely and without speculation, we can greatly increase the probability that our savings efforts will be rewarded.

Thus, the intent of this section is to show how we can apply the dual effort of saving *and* investing responsibly and realistically as a means of reaching our personal financial goals. Step one, however, is identifying your financial goals by asking and answering five core questions.

Five Core Questions

There are five questions that everyone should ask themselves to begin developing and implementing a plan to reach their financial goals. Naturally, each of the five questions must be answered to be able to implement the plan successfully. Each question, and the accompanying answer, should be written down to make a record for future reference. There will certainly be opportunities for you to refer to the questions and answers during the implementation stage of your financial plan.

As mentioned, the most common long-term financial goal for which most people save and invest is the building of a nest egg for retirement. Perhaps surprisingly, the concepts are the same when planning for the short-term financial goals as well. With short-term goals, time is not as much on your side as it is in the long term, but in most other respects, the process is nearly identical.

For many of us, especially those closer to retirement age, saving and investing for a comfortable retirement can be a major source of stress and uncertainty. For others, whether they are younger folks who don't want to begin thinking about retirement, or they are so-called high net worth individuals, these groups tend to stress over the shaky economy but take no proactive steps to mitigate their worry. But it is almost never too late or too early to establish your financial goals and set out on a course for accomplishing them.

The five key questions that follow constitute the foundation for implementing your savings and investing plan. The first thing we will do is to go over all five questions so that we can understand the impact of each of them. After that, I'll present a variety of sample situations to illustrate how these questions, and your accompanying answers, can give you sufficient direction to build whatever amount of wealth you realistically believe you can achieve. Here are the questions that I believe you should ask and answer for each financial goal you set:

1. **How much money do you need to accumulate to achieve this goal?**

2. **How much money do you have now to begin the implementation of your plan?**

3. **How many years do you expect it will take to accumulate the desired amount?**

4. **How much new money do you feel you can contribute (or save) on a regular basis (weekly, monthly, annually), to add to your plan?**

5. **What annual rate of return (compounded) will be required to allow you to accumulate the amount you desire?**

The answer to question 1 partly depends on the answer to question 3, as it involves projecting into the future. You will have to put some educated thought into how much you think you will need for retirement or what it is you saving toward.

The answer to question 2 is pretty straightforward. If you have some savings, or just received an inheritance, or just sold a house or a small business, you now have some choices as to how much of that money you want to use to start your savings and investing plan. Another situation to think about is if you are a person who has just changed jobs. Many employers give their workers information about converting your old employer retirement plan or 401(k) plan into a rollover IRA. This could easily be the source of the beginning amount for your new savings and investing financial plan.

The answer one might give for question 3 has already been addressed in my explanation of what you might answer to question 1. If you wish to save up enough money to make a down payment on a vacation home, or to put up the necessary capital to start a fast food franchise, you will need to estimate how many years it will take you to save up the necessary nest egg. There is nothing wrong with an estimate, because, in reality, if it takes a little longer or a little shorter time, you'll have made substantial progress if you stick to the plan diligently.

The answer you should come up with for question 4 will depend on you actually making a budget. The idea of saving for the future involves setting aside some portion of your income on a regular basis to contribute to your savings and investing plan. You have full control over this decision, and nobody can answer this question but you. You are limited by the amount of money you earn or receive on a regular basis. Then, you must figure out how much of that regular income can be set aside for saving without adversely jeopardizing your lifestyle and level of comfort.

The answer to question 5 is a plug figure. It is derived from a mathematical computation using the numbers provided in the answers to questions 1–4 as the first four variables, and the outcome of the computation provides the answer to question 5. In other words, it will be the ideal compounded average annual rate of return required to produce the number of dollars in your desired nest egg at the end of your saving and investing process. What is important to know is that you are in complete control of the answers to the first four questions, and from that, the answer to question 5 is simply a computation derived from your answers to the first four. You readers have several ways to access either a calculator or computer software that will allow you to do the mathematical computation to answer question 5. If neither of those is readily available to you, I have made available a link on my website to allow anyone to make that computation without any cost or fee. If you go to www.customizewallstreet.com, you will find a tab or link that says: "Answer 5 Core Questions to

Implement Your Financial Goals."

Before going any further, I need to point out one additional item about answering the five core questions. In reality, the answer to question 5 is not always going to be the "plug" figure that the mathematical computation solves. There will be certain situations where the answer to question 5 is known, meaning the annualized compounded rate of return needed to grow the invested funds to the target amount. The answer to any of the other four questions could easily be the missing variable requiring mathematical computation. For example, maybe you know the answers to questions 1, 2, 4, and 5, but need to figure out the answer to question 3—the number of years it will take to accumulate the target amount to achieve your financial goal. The same calculator or software program or link on my website can be used to calculate the answer to whichever question is the missing variable for implementing your financial plan.

It is fully expected that the first time a person runs through the five-question process that one or more of the answers will turn out to be unachievable. Maybe the required average rate of return will turn out to be too high. Maybe the amount of money you can sock away each year is just too big to handle. Or in some cases, you might discover you can contribute more to the plan than you originally budgeted. The beauty of the five questions is that they not only create a template from which you can construct your plan, but they naturally identify whether or not your plan is realistic based upon your circumstances. In any of these situations, the answer to one or more of the first four questions is simply changed to reflect a more accurate answer.

I strongly urge readers to religiously stick to whatever plan you come up with. That's the only way the plan will be successful. But that doesn't mean you cannot change the plan if reality requires it. You can modify the various numbers that comprise the answers to the five questions right at the beginning before implementation even begins. Or you can modify the variables along the way if circumstance demands it. It's like changing the time you start work each day. You can change to the night shift if it's required to keep the job or to earn a promotion. Once you make that change, you still have to go work and put in an honest day of effort. The same applies to necessary modification to the structure of your financial plan.

In the chapters with illustrations that follow, I will present a variety of scenarios, which will include examples where one of the questions other than question five will be the plug figure that needs to be computed.

As we've stated before, the process of planning for retirement is similar to that of saving and investing for any financial goal or need. The main difference between saving and investing for retirement and that for other financial goals, is that with other financial goals the amount of nest egg you acquire will probably be spent in one lump sum, instead of being withdrawn over a span of years. Retirement funds will usually be spent over your remaining life span, whereas money you've accumulated to buy a car, a vacation home, or a trip around the world will be spent in a lump sum.

The importance of this is that there is no money left after paying out the lump sum to continue to invest at a compounded rate of return. With retirement planning, there are ways to continue to grow the money you aren't withdrawing each month, so that you have the potential to keep increasing the size of your retirement nest egg as you draw from it. With other types of financial goals, where all of it used at one time, there is no continuation of the investment part of the process. This doesn't mean that you can't begin saving and investing for some new goal or project, but the one you've just accomplished is now finished.

In most other respects, saving for special projects or goals requires asking and answering the same set of five questions you would ask regarding the accumulation phase of a retirement plan. If you intend to save and invest toward a child's college education, or to start your own business potentially, you must ask all the same questions regarding the money as you would for retirement planning.

How much do you want to accumulate? How much do you have to start with? How many years do you have to grow the fund until you need the money? How much new money can you add to the fund on a periodic basis? What compounded rate of interest will it acquire to reach your target dollar amount? So let's put these five questions into practical application.

Illustration #1: Building a Nest Egg for a New Car

In the introduction to this section of the book, I explained that there are two distinct categories of financial goals for which we might wish to save and grow a nest egg. Saving for retirement is one of the categories, and that category involves two phases. I indicated that there is the accumulation phase, and then, when retirement begins, there is the spending phase.

The other category of growing a nest egg encompasses most other financial goals and dreams. In this category, the nest is likely to be spent in one lump sum, so there is generally not a spending phase stretching over a long period of time. I think we can best illustrate how the process of saving and investing works by starting with an example involving the second category of a short-term financial goal that only has the accumulation phase.

Let's begin with an example with which almost everyone can identify. In this first example, I will illustrate saving for and growing a nest egg for a young person who wants to buy a new car.

Let us imagine a young woman, Gretchen, who has recently graduated from college with a degree in marketing. After about a year of traveling abroad, she returns home to enter the job-hunting market and lands a decent, entry-level position with a starting annual salary of $36,000. After settling into her new job, and perhaps getting her living arrangements in order, she has decided she would like to buy a new car.

Many people who decide they need a new car go shopping for a car, and when they find one they want (or get sold on one by an effective car salesperson), they merely look at how much money they have, and they decide if they can afford the monthly payments on the loan.

In Gretchen's case, our new marketing employee has a more long-range approach. She is willing to set aside instant gratification and take enough time to save up money to either pay for the new car completely, or to pay enough of a down payment to make the monthly loan payments sufficiently small, so as not be a source of stress financially.

The car she wants, at today's prices, will cost about $32,000. Realizing that it might take a few years to accumulate a sizeable nest egg, she predicts that she will need approximately $35,000 by the time she can afford to buy the car of her choice. With a projected purchase price of $35,000 in her mind, she decides that she would like to accumulate the sum of $25,000, and that she would like to finance any additional amount necessary to buy a car in the category she would like.

How does she accumulate $25,000, and how long will it take? We can answer these questions with a reasonable degree of certainty if she asks herself, and ascertains the answers, to the five key questions for growing a nest egg to realize her financial goals. Here are the five questions, and her answers, for this first hypothetical illustration:

Question 1: How much money do you desire to accumulate?

Answer: The answer has already been mentioned; she wants to save for and grow a nest egg of $25,000 toward the purchase price.

Question 2: How much money do you have to start the process?

Answer: In this case, let's assume Gretchen worked while in college or perhaps received a small check as a graduation gift and that she already has $4,000 with which to start.

Question 3: Over how long a period do you hope to achieve your goal?

Answer: In this case, let's say she hopes to accumulate $25,000 within three years (thirty-six months).

Question 4: How much can you contribute on a regular basis?

Answer: Based on her earnings from her new job, Gretchen hopes to tighten her belt and contribute $400 per month for the next thirty-six months (three years).

Question 5: What compounded rate of return will it require to accumulate $25,000 by the end of the next three years?

Answer: As mentioned, the answer to this question is the plug figure. Using a financial business calculator, I can tell you that the answer is approximately 16.5% annual compounded rate.

The economic environment at the time this book is being written is such that earning a compounded rate of return of 16%, or more, is pretty unrealistic. You might ask, and with good reason, what good is this simplified plan for growing a nest egg if the result of the process requires an annual rate of return that is totally out of reach? Well, right off the bat, answering the five key questions has shown Gretchen that her goal will need some adjusting. And Gretchen has complete control over adjusting her plan for a more realistic and achievable result.

When devising a short, or especially a long-term plan, it is important to keep in mind that economic times change. A period of low-interest rates and low investment returns almost always change over time. History has proven that they do change. This book is being written to have long-lasting benefits. Where in today's environment savings accounts earn barely 1% annually, many of us remember not too many years ago when savings accounts and certificates of deposit (CDs) earned well in excess of 10% annually. As the pendulum swings, interest rates and inflation will rise again. Those of us involved in professional financial management, unfortunately, can't tell you when.

In any environment, there are usually sound investments that will deliver strong rates of return for your answer to question five. But in Gretchen's case, she is looking at a relatively short period of time—three years.

Since one of my main themes is to know and use what we can control, let's vary some of the answers in Gretchen's formula to derive a plan that reflects a more realistic annual rate of return required.

Let's suppose that our young woman, Gretchen, feels she could earn an average of 6% annually on her invested savings over the next three or four years. So, rather than the answer to question 5 being a plug figure, let's select 6% as the answer, and then make modifications to one or more of the first four questions to see if we can come up with a more realistic plan. Stated differently, we can modify one or more of the first four questions, and one of them will then become the plug figure. Here are the five questions, with modifications where possible.

Question 1: Let's assume she still wants to accumulate $25,000, so that answer will not change.

Question 2: Let's now assume that she still has exactly $4,000 to start her saving and investing program. She might think about looking through her finances for more money available to start implementing her plan. Realistically, it's probably not there. So the answer to question 2 will remain the same at $4,000.

Question 3: Let's assume that Gretchen is a realistic person. Maybe it will take a little longer than she hoped to accumulate her nest egg to buy the car of her dreams. The answer to this question (how long it will take to reach her goal) is one with which she can be flexible. So let's modify this answer from three years to three and a half years (from thirty-six months to forty-two months). If it takes an extra six months, she can live with that.

Question 4: The answer to this question (how much she will need to save monthly) now becomes the plug figure, to be computed by placing the new set of answers to questions 1, 2, 3, and 5 into our formula.

Question 5: In consideration of current economic times and the fact that she is looking to build this money over a relatively short period of time, Gretchen feels that a 6% rate of return is far more achievable than 16.5%. For the record, I tend to agree with her.

In summary, the modified variables are as follows. Gretchen will start with a sum of $4,000 and attempt to accumulate a sum of $25,000 in forty-two months (three and a half years), hoping and anticipating that her savings can be invested at an average rate of 6% annually. The plug figure will constitute the amount she needs to contribute to the plan each month for three and a half years.

Using a business calculator or a retirement planning software program, the answer to question 4 now becomes approximately $430 per month. Isn't that amazing? By expanding the time frame from three years to three and a half years, and increasing the monthly contribution by $30 from $400 to $430, she can lower the required rate of return from 16.5% to 6% annually. Obviously, 6% is a far more realistic rate of return, and she was able to reach it by making minor modifications to what she can control.

I strongly feel that working realistically with these five key questions, and modifying the answers as needed, dramatically improves your chances of achieving your financial goals. Part of this process includes focusing on what you can control, and knowing what you cannot control.

Illustration #2: Growing a College Education Fund

In this example, we are going to look at an interesting variation of a financial plan by presenting an example of building a college fund. What makes this example interesting is that it is a modified version of a lump sum financial goal required for the purchase of something, such as buying a car or placing a down payment on the purchase of a house. The concepts for building the nest egg, the saving and investing process, are basically still the same for all examples. The major difference in this example of saving for a college education is that there might be an overlapping period where the parents are still contributing into the plan while at the same time withdrawing from the plan to begin paying tuition because the child has already started attending college.

For this illustration, let's imagine a young couple in their twenties, Jared and Jennie, who've just welcomed their first child. After a while, as the novelty of parenting begins to achieve a level of normalcy, the couple begins looking to the future. Not only do they consider the question of possibly having more children, but also the challenge of planning for this child's education becomes a high priority. Let's assume that this couple feels that their neighborhood public schools are all of a sufficiently high quality (which may not be the case for families everywhere) and that their main concern is saving up for this child's college education. As an aside, they also are forward looking enough to keep in mind that whatever savings plan they establish for educating this first child will also have to be implemented in the event of future children as well.

This example will focus on accumulating a college fund for the only child they now have, but in the event of additional children, the same process can be used for each subsequent child. For now, let's go through the five-question process as it applies to saving and investing for their first child's college fund. As a preface to the planning questions and answers, we will be adding the feature that not all the money will be spent at one time. The accumulated funds will be spent over the number of years the child will be in school (i.e., college tuition and expenses will be paid out over several years of attendance rather than one lump sum.) In most typical cases, the college student will spend four years earning a degree. In reality, many students spend more than four years earning a bachelor's degree, and, in many other cases, students continue to graduate school or professional school. I will attempt to take into account some of these realities as I present this illustration. Let's get started with the five questions and answers.

Question 1: How much money do Jared and Jennie wish to accumulate for their child's college fund?

Answer: At the time this book is being written, each year of college costs anywhere from $25,000 per year (plus expenses) at typical state-funded public universities and upwards of $50,000-$60,000 at many private universities. There are a variety of situations that might reduce these massive numbers, but that would still put a quality college education out of reach for many American families without one of two funding sources. Either they would have to obtain college assistance through student loan programs, or they would have to plan far enough ahead to amass the amount needed to send one or more children to the institution of their choice.

This book is not a seminar on college loan programs, but I want to present an alternative perspective for readers who might very well be involved in planning for and paying for a child's higher education. If you choose the college loan route, either the parents or the student will face many years, in some cases decades, paying off the surprisingly astronomical costs of college. Those who choose to plan for and save up for tuition and living costs before your child enters the college market will spend years, in some cases more than a decade, paying into an education savings fund of one form or another. It is clear that paying for college by all those who don't have the ability to write four consecutive $50,000 checks will spend many years paying off college costs (either before or after). The interesting point I wish to make here is that those who choose to save and invest in building up a college nest egg before their children go to college will have the benefit of the funds earning interest or an annualized rate of return until all the funds are spent.

On the other hand, those who borrow to pay for college, and then pay back their college loans after completing their education, will not be earning interest on those funds, rather they will be paying back interest plus the amount of funds they borrowed. In other words, if you save up (and invest) the money before your child goes to college, the fund will earn interest on the investments to help build the fund. Those who pay back loans after college will be paying back more than the amount they borrowed. I hope you get it. In my opinion, it's better to earn interest than to pay interest.

For this illustration, the answer to question 1 will be an assumption that this family wishes to accumulate at least $150,000 as a college education nest egg for their first child.

Question 2: How much money do Jared and Jennie have to contribute to start the process?

Answer: Let's assume that Jared and Jennie have $5,000 to start the saving process. This being their first child, and perhaps up until the time Jennie began the pregnancy period both parents worked, and they have already accumulated a certain amount of savings.

Question 3: For how many years will Jared and Jennie save and invest until their child enters college, and they begin spending from their fund?

Answer: Note the subtle variation to this question because not all the money will be spent at once. In this example, let's assume the parents are beginning the accumulation plan when the child has her first birthday, and they expect the child will enter college when she turns eighteen years old.

As an aside comment, this does not mean that for future children they must wait until each additional child turns one year old before beginning that child's college fund. They might decide to begin each new child's fund during pregnancy, or even earlier, or perhaps when the child is older.

For this illustration, the family will begin to grow a fund from the time their child is one year old, until she reaches age eighteen, a total of seventeen years.

Question 4: How much money will the couple contribute to the education fund on a regular basis?

Answer: Naturally, the situation in each family is different, so there is no general rule as to period contributions. Let's assume in this scenario that prior to the birth of the first child both parents worked, but now one of the parents stays at home caring for the child, and will continue to do so during the preschool years of each additional child. Let's assume further that the stay-at-home parent can work from home on a part-time basis, and still contributes to the earnings income of the family.

So we will assume that the parents feel they can save $500 per month to regularly contribute to the growth of the education fund for their first child. The effect of this plan will be that they will contribute $500 per month, a total of $6,000 per year, for a total of seventeen years until the child turns eighteen years of age.

Question 5: What compounded rate of return will be required to grow a college fund of $150,000 by the end of seventeen years?

Answer: As we have seen before, the answer to this question is the plug figure, meaning it will be the figure we have to compute once the couple decides the answers to questions 1–4. To summarize, this couple wants to accumulate a total of $150,000 by the end of seventeen years by starting with a sum of $5,000, and then contributing $500 per month every month until the end of seventeen years.

The answer to question 5, the computed plug figure, is that an annual rate of return of 3.63% will be required to grow the desired nest egg amount to send their child to college in seventeen years.

In my opinion, this is a realistic and achievable annual rate of return. In fact, the required rate of return of 3.63% is a number lower than I expected it would be. Historically, the general stock market has had an annualized average rate of return exceeding 10% annually over the last seventy-five years. One could realistically expect to earn a rate of return higher than 3% or 4% annually over a seventeen-year period, based on historical averages. Maybe our couple can arrange to be a bit more aggressive in seeking a higher rate of return, and thereby grow a larger nest egg than at first anticipated without risking excess stress or uncertainty in the effort to achieve their financial goals.

Now that we've solved the rate of return required to grow the fund during the seventeen years of contributing to and growing the education fund, we want to look at the college years themselves and plan for the annual spending down of the fund. Included in this part of the exercise is determining how long the money will last, and if there will be anything left for the child to either begin life in the real world, or to extend her education into graduate or professional school.

Once again, we will ask five questions to be able to address the appropriate financial goal of having enough funds to complete the child's higher education goals. These five questions will address the spending phase of financial planning. This will differ from the spending phase in retirement planning only to the extent that with college education spending the number of years involved is usually, although not always, shorter than that of a retired person or retired couple's life expectancy.

Here are the five questions and their respective answers:

Question 1: How much money is there in the education fund for the child to begin college?

Answer: The answer from this first illustration, without any of the variations we introduced above, is the sum of $150,000. The answers to the remaining four questions will deal with how the money is distributed, and how much will be left, if any, after the college years are over.

Question 2: How many years will the fund be used to pay for the college education?

Answer: In most scenarios, people assume that college education requires four years to complete. In reality, that period is often extended beyond four years. The reason it might last more than four years is that many college students take more than four years to earn their degrees. Another common reason for extending the period is that many students continue into post-graduate studies. In this illustration, we are going to stick with the typical four years of college education.

Question 3: How much will the student withdraw for education expenses each period?

Answer: This answer is partially determined by the frequency that the student will be withdrawing from the fund. To show how the process works in a relatively realistic scenario, we will assume there will be withdrawals every six months, meaning twice each year. This would be consistent with the two-semester system at most colleges and universities. Semesters do not last a full six months, but for ease of computations, we'll make the assumption that the sufficient funds to pay for tuition, housing, and other education expenses will be withdrawn every six months.

Now we address the amount of each period withdrawal. In reality, tuition fees, as well as housing, tend to increase with the rise of inflation. Since each student's college and related expenses will differ from everyone else, we will keep the amounts of each withdrawal uniform throughout the entire four-year period. In addition, we will assume attendance at a public university, so that this illustration will not deal with the most expensive of college tuition situations. Let's assume that the entire cost of each year of education will be $40,000 per year, and that amount will remain for the next four years.

To summarize, this means that over a four-year period there will be eight withdrawals for $20,000 each from this college education fund.

Question 4: How much money would you like to have left in the fund after college is completed?

Answer: The question addresses the issue that there is life after college. There may be many reasons why the student might try to avoid using up the entire college fund that her parents, or other relatives, created on her behalf. Maybe graduate school will last longer than expected, or maybe the student would like to have money left over to assist with living expenses while looking for ideal career opportunities. If the amount left over is substantial, the student might want to be able to use it for a down payment for buying a home or car, or for starting a small business, or for the opportunity to travel before settling down.

In this illustration, let's assume that the student would like to have $20,000 left over in the fund after completing his or her years of higher education. As you can see, this might dovetail nicely with the first illustration in this section, where our young person starting a new job wanted to save up to buy a nice new car.

Question 5: What annual compounded rate of return will be required during the four years of college to have $20,000 left over?

Answer: What is hopefully apparent from these illustrations is that the investment process does not stop at the end of the accumulation period. For the fund to be fully efficient, the portion of the fund not withdrawn each period still needs to grow. To the extent possible, the funds might be invested more conservatively than during the accumulation period, so as not to expose the remaining principal fund to undue risk of loss. Since the reality of the situation is that college costs will rise with the rate of inflation, the remaining portions should continue to be invested to keep up with the impact of inflation.

As in the previous examples, the answer to question 5 is the plug figure. It is the rate of return computed from the numeric answers given to the first four questions.

Using a business calculator, the average annual compounded rate of return required to have $20,000 remaining in a fund that started with $150,000, and from which $20,000 will be withdrawn two times each year for four years, needs to be approximately 3.9% per year.

As noted in earlier examples, this percentage seems quite reasonable to achieve, considering historical average rates of return for basic investments in either stocks or bonds.

Isn't it amazing that with proper planning, financial goals can be achieved, and the part that you might have difficulty controlling—in this case, the required rate of return—might result in being a realistic, highly probable number that historically is achievable?

Wow! I think that is marvelous and promising that such a modest and realistically achievable average percentage rate of return is all that is required. One would think that an investment professional would be able to find a variety of investment choices for our couple to select from to able to deliver such investment returns.

The important thing to observe with all these illustrations is that the rates of return required to accumulate your desired nest egg are often realistic, and reasonably achievable under most market conditions. And if it is not, you, as the planner, have the ability to adjust the other four components to establish what you feel is a more reasonable rate of return. The most important variable in most cases is not the market rate of return, but the discipline of the investor, and your willingness to execute a realistic plan far enough ahead of when the funds will be needed.

Some of the variables require tough decisions followed by disciplined execution if your financial goal is going to be achieved. Computing the answer to question 5, the rate of return necessary for the plan to be successful is pretty easy. But the answer to question 4, how much money you will contribute each month, quarter, or year, creates a much greater challenge. If you say you will contribute $5,000 per year for the next twenty years, it could involve heavy discipline and sacrifice. If you lost your job five or ten years into the process, you might not have $5,000 per year for a long time to come. Worst-case scenario, your plan must be temporarily put on hold, or maybe come to a screeching halt altogether if you cannot find a new job.

It is not my purpose to create an air of doom and gloom around the idea of implementing a savings and investing plan.

The message I want to leave you with is that even in worst-case situations, you are still in charge. The answers to four of the five key questions I've presented are within your control to decide. The answer to the remaining question, whether it's question 5 or one of the other questions, is the computed plug figure that makes the plan work. And in reality, as I have shown above, you can choose a plug figure for your rate of return and work the plan in reverse.

The answers to at least four of the questions do not depend on whether the stock market goes up or down. Even if you decide not to pursue the plan at the present time, that decision, too, is within your control. Realistically, you might just have to wait until you are in a stronger position financially to implement a plan for reaching a goal you have dreamed about for a long time. When the time comes that your situation is brighter, you can pick up where you left off, and once again work on putting your plan into motion.

A FOCUS ON RETIREMENT PLANNING

The best way to illustrate how simple this financial retirement plan works is to present a couple of illustrations focused primarily on retirement planning. This type of plan is based on using the five questions in two separate time frames. The first set of five questions focuses on the period in which you are accumulating your nest egg. This is the period that can last twenty, thirty, or even more years. The second time around with the five questions, we focus on the period in which you are using the money you have accumulated, meaning the spending period during retirement years. This, too, could last several decades, because it constitutes the remainder of your lifetime. To answer this second set of questions, I will modify them just enough to be relevant to a spending period instead of an accumulation period.

For each of the following illustrations, I will present the questions and provide sample answers. My hope is that you can draw inferences and conclusions that are self-explanatory, and thereby adapt the scenarios to fit your individual needs and plans.

One of the primary reasons I am writing this book is to impart the importance of saving *and investing* for a secure retirement. I want people to better understand what they can and cannot control and to subsequently devise reasonable plans to meet their goals. One of the most powerful tools we cannot completely control is time. Young people in their twenties, thirties, and even into their forties tend to give very little attention the life-altering phenomenon of retirement. During the first three decades of adulthood (age twenty to fifty), a substantial percentage of Americans are primarily concerned with getting educated, situating themselves into their potential career paths, and building their life partnerships and their families.

Once middle age sets in, anywhere from age thirty-five to age fifty, depending on whom you're talking to, many folks suffer from a midlife crisis. This shock period often includes a reality check about retirement, whose time approaches faster than many ever thought possible. The issue of aging and planning for retirement soon leaps to the forefront. These issues manifest themselves in the form of health concerns, their related costs, and future financial security concerns. People begin to realize that their sixth and seventh decades of life are no longer a distant thought, but a fast-approaching reality.

More and more frequently these middle years are accompanied by changes in employment situations, which might increase the seriousness of planning for a financial future. They now become aware of their potential economic vulnerability if they should come to a point where they can no longer rely on income production from their working capacity.

Many folks like you and me begin to seriously ponder the point in the future where we will have to rely on revenue streams from the earnings capacity of our economic savings and capital investments. People start to ask themselves if they will have accumulated enough during their earnings years to live comfortably on nest eggs they have set aside and grown for the future.

The details of the demographics of numerous categories of Americans dealing with retirement planning, and all the related emotional issues that accompany this endeavor, will be left to works and studies of professionals more expert than myself. But I challenge anyone to contend the fact that the sooner you set and begin acting on a long-term financial plan, the better off you will be. The purpose of this section of the book is to introduce and present the concept that planning for future financial goals, especially that of a secure retirement, can be handled both sensibly and in a straightforward process by any and all of us. More importantly, and this is truly important, the process can be handled without great emotional stress and with a high probability of success for all of us.

Illustration #3: Saving and Investing for a Secure Retirement

Let's begin a fairly common illustration that will not necessarily apply to all economic demographics, but will be a scenario that most Americans can recognize even if a good percentage of the population have differing circumstances. In following illustrations, I will offer a few different scenarios that will make it apparent that almost all individuals anywhere, even those residing in other countries, can accumulate a nest egg for financial security during their twilight years.

This first of the retirement planning illustrations involves a typical married couple, where the husband is just approaching age fifty, and the wife is age forty-five. Let's further assume that both spouses derive income from productive careers outside the home. Each of them has either a modest retirement fund from either their outside employment or from having made annual contributions into an individual retirement account (IRA).

After having attended a retirement planning seminar, they now decide to get serious about saving and investing toward an additional nest egg, over and above income that will come from their various employment retirement plans and Social Security. Let's assume that they actually attended a seminar conducted by professionals who had read this book. They, and other attendees, will have been asked to list their answers to the five key questions introduced in these pages. This illustration will present some fairly generous dollar amounts, both as to amounts being started with and as to the amount of the ultimate goal. In my experience, many of the folks who attend financial planning seminars are upward in years, and have led diligent lives in both saving money and guarding against being wasteful with its use. These folks are more common in America than what is commonly suggested to the contrary.

In following examples and illustrations, I will provide scenarios for those of more modest means, but who are just as serious about wanting to save and invest for a comfortable future.

The points to focus on in this first retirement illustration is not whether the dollar amounts are larger, or smaller, than what you are used to, but that you are now seeing the basic five key questions presented in two phases.

In the first phase, we should be asking and answering five questions in the context of accumulating the nest egg for their retirement. In the second phase, the five questions, and their respective answers, are modified in the context of spending the money that has been accumulated, because the couple is retired and will be using or spending the money for the remainder of their lifetime.

Let's now ask and answer the five basic questions in two phases, first in the accumulation phase, followed by the spending phase.

The Accumulation Years

Question 1: How much money does the couple have to begin their retirement savings plan?

Answer: In this case, we indicated that our couple earns individual incomes outside the home. Their children are now grown and out of the home. We will even assume that this economically savvy couple paid for their children's college education with the help of planning, so that they do not have any heavy debt obligations facing them other than their retirement planning.

Let's further assume that each of them has contributed to their respective employers' retirement savings plans for several years, and between them, they have accumulated a total of

$100,000 in their combined qualified retirement plans from their respective employers. To make this illustration a bit simpler, let's further assume each of them has recently changed jobs, or have just started their own business, such that the $100,000 has been converted to rollover individual retirement accounts, $50,000 for her and $50,000 for him. In any event, the answer is they have $100,000.

Question 2: How much money do they wish to accumulate as a nest egg for retirement?

Answer: This couple enjoys their respective careers and anticipates working for as long as possible to build up a nest egg that will allow them the comfort of living in the style of complete comfort and enjoy the travel and hobbies of their choosing. If they keep working, they feel they can accumulate $2.0 million in a retirement fund to add to other assets they hope to have when the time comes to stop working. So the answer to question 2 is $2.0 million.

Question 3: How many years will they continue to work and contribute to their retirement nest egg?

Answer: As we stated above, the husband in this scenario is age fifty, and the wife is age forty-five. The husband feels that since they now started their own business, as long as he stays healthy he would like to keep working for the next twenty-five years, until age seventy-five. The wife has echoed that sentiment and also feels that she would like to keep working in their family business for an additional twenty-five years, until age seventy.

Now that they own their own business, an upscale family restaurant that shows signs of being very successful, they expect to contribute to self-employment retirement plans for each of them over the next twenty-five years.

Question 4: How much money will the couple contribute each year to the retirement fund?

Answer: As small business owners, the tax laws allow them to each contribute to their own qualified simplified retirement plans (often referred to as SEP-IRA accounts), and to receive tax benefits each year a contribution is made. There are contribution limits they can each make depending on the amount of their company's profit and their declared salaries.

For the sake of this illustration, let's assume that each of them can make annual contributions of $10,000 per year for the next twenty-five years. This is a total contribution for the two of them of $20,000 per year. It is assumed that they will reap tax benefits for making these contributions, but that is not the focus of this illustration. It is likewise unimportant for this scenario whether the spouses put their contributions into separate retirement accounts for each of them, or combine them into one account. The numbers will come out the same, either way.

Therefore, the answer to this question is $20,000 per year for the next twenty-five years.

Question 5: What will be the annual compounded rate of return required to reach their investment goals of $2.0 million?

Answer: By now, the readers should realize that the answer to this question, the required rate of return, is the plug figure. It is the result of a present dollar calculation by using an appropriate software program, or from using a common business calculator that computes present dollar value calculations.

To briefly review, the couple is starting with $100,000, and wishes to accumulate a total of $2.0 million by contributing $20,000 per year each year for a period of twenty-five years, and investing the funds so as to earn a compounded average annual rate of return, computed by using each of these four variables.

The answer to question 5 is a compounded rate of return of approximately 7.6% per year. At the time this book is being written, that rate of return may seem a bit higher than many people feel they can comfortably achieve. But if we look at history, studies have shown that average annual rates of return for the general stock over the last seventy-five to eighty years to be comfortably higher than 7% or 8%. In the short term, especially over the last two or three years, annual rates might not have been higher than these numbers. But over the long term, the impact of the law of averages—where the years of low returns will be offset by years of higher returns—will hopefully deliver the historical long-term average at or near the calculated average rate of return.

If adjustments are required, the couple can lower the annual rate of return by either starting with a larger amount, or by contributing a few more dollars each period, or by making contributions for a longer period of time. However, not only is the rate of return well within historically statistical averages, but also any of the adjustments they might make are within their control.

Since the planner has the control to change any of the answers to manipulate the outcome, let's change one of the variables and see how that changes the outcome of how much will be accumulated in their financial plan.

Let's just change the answer to question 5, the rate of return.

Let's assume we could control the average annual rate of return generated by our plan. I will offer two variations in the rate of return. In the first variation, we will assume that implementation of the plan will yield only a 6% average annual rate of return, compounded for twenty-five years, and all other variables remain the same.

To summarize, our couple starts with the sum of $100,000 and adds $20,000 per year for the next twenty-five years, earning an average compounded rate of return of 6%. This is a lower rate of return than our original plug figure of 7.6%. How much will they have accumulated at the end of twenty-five years with this lower rate of return? The new answer is approximately $1.5 million. Although this is not the full $2.0 million they had hoped for, it is still a hefty sum, not to be ignored or rejected.

Let's do a second modification, this time increasing the average rate of return to 8%. In summary, our couple will start with $100,000, and then add $20,000 per year for the next twenty-five years, and earn an average compounded rate of return of 8% annually. The new answer is approximately $2.1 million. It is not a large increase over the $2.0 million projected, but it illustrates the point that even small increases in some of the variables will generate additional profit.

The most important conclusion that can be drawn from this illustration is that our couple should be able to accumulate for themselves a substantial retirement nest egg, somewhere in the neighborhood of $2.0 million. No matter the actual amount they accumulate, we know they will be better off than they would have been if they had not decided to implement a plan to save and invest for their financial future.

The Withdrawal or Spending Years

A commonly overlooked aspect of financial planning and retirement is continuing to grow your retirement fund even after you begin taking withdrawals. What is fascinating about this relatively simple financial planning process is that the investment process (no matter how conservative you desire to make it) can continue, even after you retire and start withdrawing money for maintaining your desired standard of living. It can continue even after you stop making regular contributions to your plan. Many people simply neglect to address the component of continuing to allow their money to grow after the accumulation period has ended.

The process involves once again asking five key questions, the answers to which will continue to give security and comfort during the remainder of your life span. In the case of saving toward a short-term financial goal such as a down payment for a house, there is no need to address the withdrawal period because the nest egg is paid out in a lump sum. But remember that if a person is saving for a short-term financial goal such as someone's college education, the amount accumulated will be spent over a period ranging anywhere from four to ten years, so there is a withdrawal period where some of the accumulated money can continue to grow.

For this illustration, let's continue to consider the case of a retirement plan, though the principles can apply to any financial goal that includes spending accumulated money over an extended period of time.

As we did above, we now present the five key questions one should ask, and answer, related to the period during which you will be spending the money you worked so hard to accumulate. The five questions are surprisingly similar. Here they are:

One: How much money have you accumulated that is now available for withdrawal?

Two: How much money do you want or need to withdraw each period (weekly, monthly, quarterly)?

Three: How much time (months, years, decades) do you expect to be taking regular withdrawals?

Four: How much money do you expect or want to have left, if any, at the end of the withdrawal period (months, years, life expectancy) to leave to heirs or apply to another financial purpose?

Five: What annual rate of return (compounded) will you need to maintain on average during the withdrawal period to achieve your goal?

Once again, the answer to question five is a plug figure that requires a business calculator or software program to compute. The answers to the first four questions are completely within your control, as they were in the first phase of the planning process.

Some of the answers may involve educated guessing, because no one can predict the future. Making assumptions and answering questions based on your best estimates and life expectations is appropriate. You would have to do that in any case, even if you engaged a financial professional to prepare a formal financial, multipage financial plan for you. In fact, one of those detailed, extensive, financial plans might go off in so many directions that they distract you from focusing on the core information you need to know for successful financial planning.

There is one more benefit to the process I am presenting.

There are no right or wrong answers to the questions, in either the accumulation phase or the withdrawal phase. If the answer to question five, the plug figure, ends up to be a clearly unrealistic or unachievable number, the answers to the other questions simply need to be adjusted to reflect a more realistic result. Simply being honest with what you can and cannot control, and honest with what is realistic and unrealistic, will provide you with the answers and plan you need to address your personal goals and situation.

Additionally, you can (and should) monitor the progress of the plan along the way, as well as the features of the plan you can control. Perhaps circumstances change that makes the original plan too aggressive or too conservative. This can easily happen if you realize you have more or less money to regularly contribute, more or less time to save, etc. The point is that you are not only in control of creating the initial plan, but in monitoring the five simple questions and making sound adjustments along the way.

Our retirement-planning couple wants to know the whole picture about the potential of their retirement plan. They not only want to know what it will take to accumulate the desired $2.0 million, but they also want to know how long it will last once they commence spending it during their retirement years. They would also like to know if there will be any amount left over, depending on when the second of them passes away, to leave as an inheritance to their children or heirs.

To give projected answers (they certainly cannot be promises) to our couple, we once again ask five key questions. This version of the questions will have a withdrawal or spending orientation, as opposed to a contribution or accumulation orientation, which was apparent in the first set of five questions. So, let's again ask our five basic questions:

One: How much money does our couple have to begin the withdrawal phase of their retirement?

Answer: The answer to this question takes over where the last set of five questions left off. We will assume that our couple was successful in implementing the accumulation phase of their retirement plan with a 7.6% rate of return. That being the case, the answer to question 1 is that they have the sum of $2.0 million to begin the withdrawal phase of their retirement plan.

Two: How many years do they plan to withdraw and spend from their retirement fund?

Answer: As has been suggested before, the number of years one plans to withdraw money from a retirement nest egg is going to depend on life expectancies. In the illustration, the husband is age seventy-five at the beginning of retirement, and the wife is age seventy. Even though we are dealing with two people, and therefore two different life expectancies, we will answer this question based on the age of the younger of the two spouses. So, for this illustration, let's assume that each spouse will live until age ninety-five. With the wife being age seventy at the beginning of the retirement fund withdrawal period, the answer to this question is twenty-five years.

Three: How much money does our couple wish (or need) to withdraw from their nest egg on a regular basis?

Answer: The answer to this question depends on additional variables unique to each individual situation. Various questions need to be answered to determine how much our couple will withdraw monthly, quarterly, or annually. How much other income do they receive, such as Social Security, employer-sponsored retirement plans, and perhaps income from other investments? How much are their monthly obligations? Do they still pay a monthly mortgage, or heavy rent payments? Do they have high travel expenses, or other luxuries, or support other family members?

In this illustration, let's assume that our couple wishes to withdraw $6,000 per month, a total of $72,000 per year. They probably arrived at this figure by looking at all their other sources of income, and their monetary needs based on the standard of living to which they are accustomed. Perhaps one or both spouses receive payments from an employment retirement plan. Adding all these amounts to the Social Security payments they might be receiving gives them a level of monthly and an annual income that hopefully makes their standard of living comfortable. On the spending side, besides their usual costs of living, perhaps they support an elderly parent who is still living, or supporting one or more children who need financial assistance, or quite common in many families, they are funding college educations for their grandchildren. Based on all these considerations, different for all families, they arrived at an amount they wish to withdraw from their accumulated nest egg each month.

Now, let's assume the above amount of withdrawals will continue in the same amount for the full twenty-five years, whether both spouses are living, or only one still survives. The answer to question three is $72,000 per year.

Four: How much money does our couple desire to have left over or leave as an inheritance to their heirs?

Answer: The answer to this question depends not only on how much money our couple withdraws and spends over their remaining lifetimes, but it also depends on the rate of return that the funds not yet withdrawn will earn on an annual basis. The rate of return question will be addressed in question 5. For now, let's assume our couple wishes to leave an inheritance to their children of $1.5 million.

Five: What compounded annual rate of return is required to have a remaining balance of $1.5 million?

Answer: The answer to this question is again computed as a plug figure, just as with the other illustrations. In this case, the amounts in the retirement fund not yet withdrawn each year is invested, so that it continues to grow. The couple hopes they will not outlive their retirement nest egg, and that there might be enough left over as an inheritance for their heirs.

To have a sum of $1.5 million left for their children or other heirs, what rate of return will be required? To summarize the variables, our couple is beginning their retirement withdrawal phase with $2.0 million, from which they plan to withdraw at the rate of $72,000 annually, for a joint life expectancy period of twenty-five years. They hope to have $1.5 million remaining to bequeath to others. The answer to question 5 is a conservative rate of return of approximately 2.9% annually.

Our couple should have little problem finding conservative investments that historically have delivered average annual rates of return in the range of 3%.

Maybe our couple wishes to modify some of the variables to see if they can withdraw more money annually and still leave a nice inheritance to their children. What if we modify the answer to question 3, and the couple decides they wish to withdraw $100,000 every year for the expected twenty-five-year period? What would be the required rate of return if they made that change? Now the variables will be those of starting with $2.0 million, and withdrawing $100,000 per year for a period of twenty-five years, and desiring to have the sum of $1.5million remaining for their heirs. With these changes, the answer to question 5 increases to approximately 4.4% per year. Even with this change, our couple should be able to find conservative investments that return between 4% and 5% annually, without exposing the principal to substantial risk of loss.

Before we leave this illustration, I want to point out one more variation. What if the couple doesn't live the expected twenty-five years? How does that change the outcome? I will illustrate this by returning to the original set of variables, where the annual withdrawal was $72,000 per year. Now, let's change the answer to question 2 to be fifteen years instead of twenty-five years. It is realistic that both spouses could die before their estimated life expectancies. The usage of their retirement funds would cease.

To summarize this modified illustration, our couple started the spending phase with $2.0 million, and withdrew $72,000 per year for a period of fifteen years with the plan to have $1.5 million left for their heirs upon death. What average compounded rate of return on the portion of the assets not yet withdrawn would be required? This number is once again the plug figure answer to question 5. The answer is computed to be approximately 2.2% annual rate of return. The mathematics of the computation and significant decrease in the rate of return was influenced by both the fact that the time period was shorter, and the fact that the number of $72,000 withdrawals was also reduced by ten years.

As we conclude this illustration, it is interesting to point out that in all variations we have shown here, the required rate of return in both the accumulation phases and in the withdrawal phases were realistically achievable in comparison to what you might expect before doing the mathematical calculation.

My purpose with these illustrations is to once again focus on those variables that you can control. In many instances, some of them quite surprising, the variables over which we have no control might realistically turn out well within our reach. If required rates of return are well below historical averages, then maybe the levels of stress for using the stock market or other investment categories can be substantially reduced.

Illustration #4: Another Retirement Example

In this example, let's look at a more modestly situated individual to see if they can grow a retirement nest egg that will sufficiently allow them to achieve a useful retirement fund, so as to live out the retirement years in comfort and without stress or worry.

In this illustration, we will focus on a thirty-five-year old man, who has an engineering degree and does structural design work for a real estate development company. Furthermore, he is a single dad who shares custody of his nine-year-old daughter with his ex-wife. The daughter lives with him half of the time, and because the child's mother has a good job he pays her no alimony, and his monthly child support payments still leave him enough to begin saving and investing toward a retirement nest egg.

Our saver-investor, Tom, earns about $70,000 annually, and

he feels that he can set aside enough each year to take advantage of the IRA maximum deduction per year to build up his retirement fund. Note that our investor may or may not get a tax deduction for the amount he saves for his retirement nest egg, depending on whether his employment has a qualified plan in which he participates. For purposes of this illustration, let's assume he does not have a retirement plan at his place of employment. The maximum tax deduction for individual retirement accounts by a single person in the year this book is written, for contributors under age fifty, is $5,000 per year.

We will now go through our five retirement plan questions and answers for the accumulation years, and then follow with the five questions and answers for the withdrawal years.

One: How much money does Tom have now with which to begin his retirement saving and investing plan?

Answer: As has been already stated, our thirty-five-year-old single parent has a relatively good job, and he is careful with his personal spending and budgeting. Let's assume he will begin his accumulation phase toward a retirement nest egg with $5,000 already saved.

Two: How much money would Tom like to accumulate as a retirement nest egg?

Answer: Tom knows that retirement is many years away. He understands that the effects of inflation over twenty or thirty years can whittle away the purchasing power of his savings, so he knows he must accumulate a sufficient amount to offset its negative effects. He decides that he would be wise to grow a nest egg of at least $1.5 million by the time he finally stops working.

This seems like a rather large amount to accumulate, but he wants to know if he has a reasonable chance to do so if he is diligent and disciplined.

Three: How much money is Tom willing/able to contribute each year to his retirement saving and investing plan?

Answer: As we stated in the introductory paragraph to this illustration, our single parent wishes to contribute the maximum amount that gives him a tax deduction for contributing to a qualified IRA investment account. During the year of publication of the first edition of this book, that amount is $5,000 per year for a person thirty-five years of age.

(It should be noted that in recent years, Congress has increased the amount of IRA annual deductions to keep up with inflation. So our investor will be able to increase his contributions whenever that occurs again, and if he can afford to do so.)

Another way he will be able to increase contributions in the future is that under current regulations, when he reaches age fifty, he will be able to contribute $6,000 annually to an IRA investment account. With the occasional cost of living increases, by the time he reaches age fifty (in fifteen years), the deductible amount might be even larger. For now, the answer to this question is $5,000 per year.

Four: For how many years will Tom make his annual contributions toward his retirement plan?

Answer: Our investor-saver, Tom, knows that people are living longer, staying healthier longer, and working longer than in prior generations. He knows that the longer he works, if he's healthy, the greater chance he will have of reaching his financial goals. At this time, he feels he would like to work until age seventy, especially if he finds it rewarding to do so. Therefore, he plans to make annual contributions to his retirement plan for the next thirty-five years.

Five: What compounded average annual rate of return will be needed to grow Tom's nest egg to $1.5 million?

Answer: From the answers to the first four questions we've asked, we know that our investor-saver wishes to accumulate a retirement nest egg of $1.5 million by starting with a sum of $5,000, and then continuously contributing an additional $5,000 every year for the next thirty-five years. To achieve that goal, his growing nest egg must earn an average annual compounded rate of return of almost exactly 10% per year, for the entire thirty-five-year period.

Based on current annual rates of return, an annual rate of return of 10% might be viewed by most conservative investors as being unrealistic. Historical statistics suggest that investments in large company stocks have averaged just about 10% annually, on average, over the last eighty-five years. Naturally, there are numerous variables that come into play when investing over eighty-five years, or in this case, over thirty-five years. There is no way that any economist or professional portfolio manager can guarantee or even rationally encourage the possibility that an investor will comfortably earn an average return of 10% over the next three or four decades.

What is important about this computation is that our saver-investor can look at the big picture, and perhaps decide what variables he can control and not control, as well as which variables he has the power to change or not change.

For example, if he adjusts just two of the answers to the first four questions, his task might look substantially more achievable, based on historical stock market returns and current economic conditions. If he lowers the amount he expects to grow his retirement fund to $1.2 million, and if he increases the amount he can save each year to $6,000 per year for thirty-five years, the required annual rate of return will be lowered to approximately 8.4% annually.

The probability of finding consistent investments that return 8% or 9% is higher than finding 10% returns. There are no guarantees, but the fact that there are ways to make retirement planning, saving, and investing less stressful, is the key message here. In the illustration we are now discussing, we have not even added in the variable that our single parent might enjoy increased annual income over the years, consistent with the rise of inflation, which will allow him to increase his annual contributions along the way.

The recurring message is that the most important variables are those that the individual can control. If a person has the motivation, the desire, the discipline, and the consistent habit of saving and investing wisely for their financial future, there are ways to do so wisely and conservatively.

The Withdrawal or Spending Years Revisited

Now that Tom has accumulated a retirement nest egg, we will look at the spending or withdrawal phase of a retirement plan. As with the college education plan and retirement couple, there is a spending or withdrawal phase to many savings plans and nearly all retirement plans. In most situations, individuals might have two goals with their retirement nest egg.

Their first objective is not to run out of money during their retirement years. For many folks, the second objective is to have money left over to leave an estate to their children or other heirs. To address these concerns, we again ask five questions, modified slightly to account for the lack of additional contributions, and to account for the fact that there will be withdrawals from the nest egg.

Let's jump forward thirty-five years to when Tom is seventy and ready to enter his retirement period, when money is now going to be withdrawn, and accumulation will no longer take place. Let's go through the five questions that apply to this spending phase of retirement.

One: How much money does Tom have to begin his retirement years?

Answer: Let's be optimistic, and answer this question by concluding that Tom was able to average the 8.4% rate of return over the thirty-five years and put that extra $1,000 per year aside to build the $1.2 million retirement nest egg. We will take one additional liberty with the answer to this question. Let's assume there are some additional funds that our individual has available, such as the proceeds from the sale of a house, or monthly Social Security payments, or an inheritance along the way from his parents or other relatives.

What we're adding here, for purposes of this illustration, is that the accumulation of the $1.2 million nest egg is the additional money to make his life more comfortable during retirement, the ability to enjoy some of the extras in life after having worked hard for the last thirty-five years.

Two: For how many years will Tom make withdrawals from his nest egg?

Answer: Again, the answer here is a bit subjective and is basically an estimate of life expectancy. The withdrawal period is slated to begin when Tom turns seventy. Without the use of an actual statistician for this exercise, let's assume that Tom will live an additional twenty-five years, until age ninety-five. In real life, there are numerous variables such as health, genetic makeup, and other factors that could lengthen or shorten life expectancy. We will use twenty-five years to allow us to illustrate how this retirement spending phase fits into the planning process.

Three: How much money will Tom wish to withdraw each year during his retirement?

Answer: As we have previously discussed the variables that can impact this answer, and for purposes of the illustration at hand, let's use a figure of $5,000 per month for his cost of living, which totals $60,000 per year that our investor will seek to withdraw during the spending years of retirement.

Four: How much money (if any) does Tom wish to have at the end of his lifetime to perhaps pass on to his daughter or grandchildren?

Answer: It is by no means a requirement that our individual provide an inheritance for his surviving family. However, most people desire to leave some type of legacy, whether to loved ones or perhaps to a charity. So at the very least, the question should be asked that we have a figure, zero or greater, to plan for and plug in.

In this instance, let's assume our individual thinks it would be nice if he could leave an inheritance of at least $750,000 at his death, to make life a little easier for his child and his family.

Five: What average annual compounded rate of return will be required for Tom to have $750,000 left at the end of his lifetime?

Answer: Once again using the calculator, we will summarize the variables we have to calculate the annual rate of return. Our single father, Tom, will commence retirement with $1.2 million, and withdraw $60,000 per year for an expected twenty-five years, and hope to have $750,000 remaining, assuming he dies at the end of those twenty-five years.

For this group of assumptions, the average annual compounded rate of return required on all the funds not withdrawn from the retirement fund will be approximately 4.1% annually.

As has been pointed out several times, an average annual return of investments in the general stock market is well above the 4% or 5% level, historically, for the last eighty or more years. Perhaps our individual could be a bit more generous in one or more of the variables and still keep the required rate of return at a relatively conservative level.

What if Tom decides he would like to receive $6,000 per month, which would be $72,000 per year, over the twenty-five years of remaining life expectancy, and that he would like to have an estate of $1.0 million to leave to his child's family? What would the average annual compounded rate of return be if he has $1.2 million to begin his retirement years? The answer to question five, based on these modified assumptions, would be approximately 5.7%. Again, it appears that the annual rate of return would still be sufficiently realistic, based on historical stock market returns, to allow him to enter into such a plan.

Introducing Multiple Financial Goals

In real life, a family will usually have a combination of financial needs or goals for which they need to save that come and go throughout their lifetime. Can the concept of saving and investing toward your financial goal, such as retirement, be applied to growing more than one nest egg simultaneously? The answer is an emphatic yes.

The only difference in financial planning for multiple goals or needs is that the five questions you ask might have to be segmented for the differing time frames and differing dollar amounts needed for each financial purpose. Although the planning process, and the separate groups of five questions can appear to be complex at first, it does not have to be.

The most direct approach I think works best for this illustration will be to apply our questions to a multilayered scenario so that you can see how the process works when you have more than one financial goal.

Illustration # 5: Planning for Three Financial Goals

First, let's set the scene for this illustration. Assume we have a young family. The husband and wife are both age thirty, and they have one child, a six-year-old daughter. They do not plan on having any more children. Assume both spouses are currently employed, one being a public school teacher, and the other a computer software systems analyst working for a major technology firm. They recently sat down and decided to become more organized in planning for their future financial needs.

The young couple identified three basic financial goals for which they would like to save and invest. After some discussion and thought, they concluded that each of the goals has equal importance, but the timing for their respective monetary needs are different. The three financial nest eggs, in order of time they need the money, are as follows:

- Saving up for a down payment to purchase a family home

- Building a nest egg to pay for their daughter's college education

- Accumulating retirement savings, over and above any amounts they will receive from their respective employments and Social Security

On the surface, this process of building a nest egg to cover three different financial needs could be somewhat complex—perhaps overwhelming. A basic approach could be, just save as much as you can as often as you can. No problem, no analysis required. But, as we have already discussed, *saving* is only half of the equation when it comes to building your nest egg for the future.

In reality, you should create a plan that allows for the following: 1) you need to feel a sense of confidence that you can achieve your financial goals, 2) you need a clear-cut idea of how to implement your savings and investing plan, 3) you will be more successful if you can eliminate stress by recognizing factors you can and cannot control in the implementation process, and 4) you should have the ability and knowledge to monitor your progress.

With financial needs that will come about at different stages in our lives, the process of saving and investing can be daunting and complex. Having been in these various situations personally in my life, I feel that using the approach of our five basic questions can demystify and simplify the process.

There are two possible approaches to this process, neither of which is better than the other. It depends on how you want to handle them, in that they both ultimately end up with the same result. It all depends on the comfort level of the people concerned. I encourage you to consider both and decide what works best for you. Let's begin the process.

Under both approaches, we first need to determine the amounts needed to fund each financial project or goal, and the timing of those needs. In this example, it would seem apparent that the first financial need would be the down payment for their new house. In this case, let's assume that will be in the next three to five years. The second of their financial needs will be for payment of their child's college education. Their six-year-old daughter will likely enter college in twelve years at age eighteen. If the couple had more than one child, saving and investing for a college fund could be viewed as a separate project for as many children as there are in the family. In this case, we have simplified the process by assuming just one child in the family. The third and final financial goal will be the accumulation of a retirement nest egg for our couple, over and above any funds provided from employer-sponsored plans or Social Security. Saving up for a retirement nest egg for two spouses could be divided into two separate funding projects, because there are two working spouses. This would especially be true if the spouses are of different ages, and plan to retire in different years. Again, to avoid additional confusion and complexity, we will assume that both spouses have professional employment, that they are both thirty years of age, and that they both intend to retire at age sixty-five. That will be in thirty-five years.

Earlier, I stated that we could use one of two possible approaches to developing and implementing a saving and investing plan for these three financial goals. One method would be to treat each of the goals separate from the others, and to handle them one at a time on a sequential basis. In other words, the couple would begin saving and investing to accumulate the required down payment for their house, and for only that project. Once that project is completed, they could then begin the process of accumulating and growing the college education nest egg, and work on that alone. Finally, once that second project is completed, they could finally begin saving and investing for their desired retirement nest egg.

A second approach would be to combine all three projects in a way that from the very beginning, they are saving and investing for all three financial goals together. As the time frame occurs for each of the three projects, they could withdraw the necessary amounts to fund each of their needs, while continuing to grow the nest eggs for the projects that will come up later.

The benefit of the first approach is that some people like to do one thing at a time. They may have limited resources, and don't want to spread themselves so thin that they run the risk of not achieving any of their goals. They may want to narrow their focus to ensure completion of the goal at hand before commencing another. The downside of completing one project at a time is that all three projects might have equal importance. They will have to choose which one to do first, and the others will just have to wait, even though the ones waiting are just as important.

The advantage of using the second approach is that each project will be completed in its natural time frame, without having to be put on hold waiting for completion of other projects deemed more important. This second approach can only be used if the parties feel they have enough monetary resources and personal energy to work on more than one project at a time. The negative to the multitasking approach is that the parties run the risk of not achieving any of their goals because of spreading themselves too thin.

Because the first approach is nothing more than a sequential application of illustrations I've already presented in earlier chapters, I feel it would be more advantageous to use this opportunity to look at the second approach.

As a reminder, if our couple decides to use the first method, the key point you should understand is that our couple would ask and answer the five basic questions for each project on a one-at-a-time basis. They would not begin to ask the five questions related to the second project until they finalize the accumulation process for the first project, thus keeping them separate.

The example I will present for this illustration will use the second approach of combining all three projects. Generally speaking, we will be taking a big picture approach to begin the process, and then narrow it down to the specific needs of each project.

First, we want our couple to think about it and estimate the total amount of dollars they feel they will need to complete all three projects combined. Using the big picture approach, we will ask the five basic questions related to the accumulation phase as if the three projects were just one big financial plan, extending in time from the beginning of the first of the projects, and lasting until the end of the accumulation phase of the third project.

When we have the answers to all five basic questions, we will then break it all down and answer the five questions separately for each of the three projects.

Applying the Five Key Questions to All Three Goals Combined

Question 1: How much money does the couple have to begin saving and investing for these three financial goals?

Answer: This young couple is embarking on an ambitious series of financial goals, and they know they have to be diligent and focused to be successful with all three projects. In this case, they have been talking and planning for these things for several years. Luckily, they are not just now beginning to save; they have already been doing that for several years. What they are doing now is becoming more focused by implementing a plan that will allow them to monitor their progress along the way.

Because of their goods jobs, and their disciplined approach to saving, we will assume this couple already has saved $40,000 with which to start accumulating a nest egg toward these three financial goals.

Question 2: How much money does our couple wish to accumulate to be able to fulfill all three financial goals?

Answer: Using this big picture approach, here is where we add up the total of all three projects to determine the total amount needed to achieve the couple's financial goals. They want to accumulate enough money over time to make a substantial down payment on a new house; they want to have enough money to send their child to college; and finally, they want to accumulate enough money for a comfortable retirement, over and above what will be provided by Social Security and their employers' retirement plans.

The cost of purchasing a new single family residence at the time of the writing of this book is substantially lower than it was three or four years earlier at the height of the real estate market around 2005–2007. If the couple lives in Southern California or other high-priced metropolitan areas like New York City or Chicago, housing is still relatively expensive for most young couples with children. Single family residences in suburban areas around the more expensive real estate markets still cost in excess of $1.0 million. These prices might be out of reach for our young couple.

For purposes of this illustration, let us assume they plan to purchase a residence that will be priced at $500,000, and that they will want to make a down payment of $100,000, which is 20% of the purchase price.

The next item they will be saving for is their child's college education. Their daughter should be ready to enter college in twelve years. It would be a speculative endeavor to be able to factor in the impact of inflation on the cost of higher education in the coming twelve years. We will just use today's estimated numbers for the cost of private university education, and if actual dollar amounts are different, our couple can make adjustments along the way. For purposes of this illustration, we will assume that the annual cost of college education at a private university is $50,000. Although most parents want their children to finish and earn their degrees in four years, the reality is that many students take five years to complete their education. So in this example, we will allow for an extra year of education. Even if the daughter finishes in four years, by accumulating funding for five years, it will allow for the possible cost of living increases that could easily impact the true cost of education twelve years down the road. The total amount our couple desires to accumulate, as a college fund, will be $300,000. This will represent college costs of $50,000 per year for up to six years. If their daughter graduate in less, perhaps they can help out with graduate school.

The first tuition payment will commence in twelve years, when the daughter is age eighteen. The rest of the college fund will be used at the rate of $50,000 per year for either the following three years to five years. Nevertheless, to keep this illustration straightforward, we will assume the full amount of $300,000 will be accumulated by the end of twelve years. It makes no difference if the full amount is spent all in one year, or spread over four to six years.

The third and final financial goal our couple will save and invest for will be a retirement fund, to hopefully make them more secure and comfortable than relying only on Social Security and the retirement plans from their employment. They understand that with the impact of inflation the purchasing power of today's dollar will be much lower in thirty-five years when they plan to retire. Without being overly scientific or mathematically accurate, they feel that if they save and grow a retirement fund to an amount equaling $1.6 million, they will feel quite successful with a nest egg of that size. As the economic climate changes over the years, they feel they will be able to adjust their target goals whenever needed.

In summary, the answer to question 2, how much money do they wish to accumulate, will be the total for all three projects, which will be a $100,000 down payment, plus a $300,000 college fund, plus a $1.6 million retirement nest egg. The total amount to be saved and invested equals $2.0 million.

Question 3: How many years will it take to accumulate enough money to fulfill all three financial goals?

Answer: The answer to this question can be a bit complex and confusing. On the surface, the answer is thirty-five years. That is when the final goal of retiring at age sixty-five for both spouses will occur. What complicates the situation is that portions of the nest egg will be spent along the way. $100,000 will be spent in three years as a down payment for the couple's first home. After that, $50,000 per year for up to six years will be spent when their daughter goes to college and maybe grad school. Eventually, after thirty-five years have transpired, retirement will begin, and the balance of their nest egg will hopefully fund their retirement for the rest of their lives.

For now, since the total amount needed for all three projects will be the sum of $2.0 million, let us begin the analysis in the first round of asking and answering the basic five questions, by assuming that the full thirty-five years will be used to accumulate $2.0 million. Under this approach, the answer to question 3 is thirty-five years.

Question 4: How much will our couple contribute each year to achieve their three desired financial goals?

Answer: The answer to this question will require a bit of thought. Our couple desires a total amount of $2.0 million to be accumulated as a total nest egg over a thirty-five-year period. Realistically, the couple will need the first $100,000 in the next three years to use as the down payment to purchase their first home. Another $50,000 per year will be needed starting in twelve years, with the same amount being needed each year thereafter for a period of six years, for their daughter's tuition payments.

The balance of $1.65 million will be used beginning in thirty-five years to fund their retirement years.

There are only two considerations our couple will keep in mind when deciding how much they will contribute each year toward accumulating their desired financial nest egg. They need to select an amount they wish to set aside each year, on a consistent, disciplined basis. They must also be realistic, and decide how much they can afford to set aside each year, because, in reality, most people want to save for retirement, but they don't want to reduce their standard of living along the way.

Our couple is fortunate. Even though they are relatively young, they both have good income from their jobs, one being a schoolteacher and the other a middle executive in a successful high-tech firm. In considering what they can afford to set aside each month, they feel they have the discipline to save $1,500 per month (a total of $18,000 per year) for the foreseeable future. They decided that each of them would try to contribute $750 per month from their individual salaries.

They also feel committed to being able to save this amount on a monthly basis and that they can keep it up for all thirty-five years. Will that be enough for them to achieve their goal of $2.0 million? If they earn no percentage on their savings, it will not accumulate to the amount they desire. Setting aside $1,500 per month for a period of thirty-five years (420 months) will yield a total of $630,000. That sum alone, even with the addition of the $40,000 they are starting with, only accounts for about one-third of the $2.0 million they feel they will need.

Therefore, the answer to question 4 is that $18,000 per year will be contributed to achieving the couple's financial goals. That amount will remain the same for all three financial goals, whether we use the combined approach or the individual project approach, for implementing the saving and investing process.

Question 5: What annual compounded rate of return will be required for the couple to achieve their stated financial goals?

Answer: As we do with each illustration, let's summarize what variables we will use to compute the answer to question 5, the required rate of return. In this instance, our couple will start with a sum of $40,000, and then make monthly contributions of $1,500 per month (a total of $18,000 annually) each month for a period of thirty-five years (a total of 420 months). They hope to accumulate a total nest egg of $2.0 million, from which various amounts totaling $350,000 ($100,000 for down payment on a house, and $300,000 for their child's college education) will be withdrawn along the way, prior to the end of thirty-five years. The remaining sum of $1.65 million is desired to be accumulated for funding their retirement in thirty-five years.

For an initial answer to question 5, we will ignore withdrawals at various stages along the way. The answer to question 5, the required average annual compounded rate of return on the money as it accumulates, using the calculator or software program we've referred to earlier, is approximately 5.6%.

Separating the Three Financial Goals

As we have observed in several previous examples, an average rate of return of 5.6% is realistic and has a high probability, historically, of being achieved over a thirty-five-year period. If that is indeed the case, then our approach of combining all three projects, for purposes of analysis, is complete. Now, let's turn to the approach where we deal with each of the three projects individually.

Accumulating a Down Payment to Purchase a New House

Let's run through the five key questions for each project. We will answer them sequentially based on time. The first goal will be accumulating enough money to make a down payment on the couple's first house. Here are the five questions:

Question 1: How much money does the couple have to begin accumulating a down payment?

Answer: The couple has a beginning amount of $40,000 to commence implementation of the first of their three projects. Remember, the answers to the remaining four questions of this first project will now be different than when the projects were combined, because of the shorter time period toward this more immediate goal.

Question 2: How much money does our couple want to accumulate for their down payment?

Answer: Based on projected suburban home prices in the next three to five years, they anticipate having to pay $500,000 to purchase a single family residence in a neighborhood they would enjoy. They will need to accumulate a sum of $100,000 to make a 20% down payment.

Question 3: How many years will it take to accumulate the desired down payment?

Answer: When we use this approach of addressing each project separately, the answer to this question becomes the plug figure. That means this is the variable we solve for, after providing the answers to the other four questions. I will give you a hint now: the answer to question 5, the rate of return percentage, will already be answered. We are going to use the same percentage that was computed when using the combined approach to all three projects. Since we already came up with a realistic and fair answer to the rate of return required, there is no reason for that to change. Using the same figure of 5.6% as our average compounded rate of return, we will be able to conclude the answer to this question 3 – how many years it will take to accumulate $100,000 down payment for the purchase of their house.

To keep you in suspense (just for a short while), we'll go ahead and answer questions 4 and 5 now, and then return to question 3 to calculate the plug figure, the number of years it will take.

Question 4: How much money does our couple plan to contribute each year toward their financial goals?

Answer: The answer to this question will not change from the answer to question 4 in the above combined approach. They have decided that they can afford to contribute an amount of $1,500 per month ($18,000 per year) toward implementation of their financial plan. That same amount will apply to each of their three projects, no matter if the projects are approached jointly, as we've already done, or if they are approached separately, as we are doing now.

Question 5: What is the compounded annual rate of return that will be required?

Answer: As I indicated a bit earlier, once we computed an average compounded rate of return of 5.6% using the combined approach, there is no reason to change that rate of return. If we stick to that answer for question 5, in each of the three separate projects, then we have the opportunity to select the answer to one of the other four questions to be calculated as the plug figure.

So let's revisit question 3. As we have done in previous illustrations, let's summarize the answers to the other variables. Our couple is starting with $40,000, and they wish to accumulate $100,000 to use as a down payment. They will contribute the sum of $18,000 per year (in increments of $1,500 per month) to their saving and investing plan. They hope to earn an average compounded rate of return of 5.6% during the accumulation period.

The answer to the question as to how long it will take to accumulate $100,000 is approximately three years. Actually, if our couple makes contributions of $1,500 every month ($18,000 per year), and if the contributions are being invested wisely every month, the effect of monthly compounding over a full three years (thirty-six months) will result in the accumulation of approximately $105,000, rather than just $100,000.

For purposes of this three-project approach, we will assume there is $5,000 left over at the end of the first three years, after our couple accumulated the down payment for their house.

Accumulating a College Education Nest Egg

Now our couple wishes to focus on their second financial goal of accumulating a nest egg for sending their daughter to college. Their goal in this project is to accumulate a total of $300,000 to cover approximately $50,000 per year for up to six years of undergraduate college studies, plus enough excess to allow for additional two years of graduate school.

Their daughter was six years old when the first project of saving up for a down payment on a house began. Now, three years later, their daughter is nine years old. Let's assume that she plans to enter college right after finishing high school, at the age of eighteen, which will be nine years from the beginning of this second project. To keep this illustration as uncomplicated as possible, let's also assume that our couple plans to accumulate the entire $300,000 by the time their daughter enters college, if they can. So they will try to accumulate the full $300,000 in the next nine years. If it takes them longer, they hope to be able to accumulate the full amount at least before their daughter finishes college and graduate school, if she so chooses.

We are now ready to address our basic five questions for this second project of accumulating a college fund for their daughter. We will quickly go through them to determine how long it will take to accumulate $300,000. To decide how long it will take to build a $300,000 nest egg, we can assume that the answers to some of the other questions will remain the same as they were in the first project, saving for a down payment.

Question 1: How much money does the couple have to begin saving toward college?

Answer: Now that the first three years have gone by, and our couple has made the down payment for the purchase of a home, they will begin the saving and investing process for building a college fund for their child.

When we revisited the answer to question 3 in the first project of accumulating a down payment, we calculated that our couple raised $105,000 in three years. Assuming they spent exactly $100,000 as their down payment for their new house, which left an excess of $5,000 that they did not spend.

As a result, the answer to this question for this second project of accumulating funds for their daughter's college education is the sum of $5,000. They will begin the process of accumulating $300,000 with the amount of $5,000.

Question 2: We know that our couple wishes to accumulate $300,000 over the next nine years to provide funding for four years of undergraduate college education, plus the ability for her to attend up to two years of graduate school.

Question 3: As was the case with the house down payments, the answer to question three is what we will be solving as the plug in.

Question 4: We know that our couple is dedicated to contributing $1,500 per month toward implementation of their three financial goals.

Question 5: We also know that the couple is comfortable planning for the rate of return to be approximately 5.6% per year.

We can now revisit question 3 by using a rate of return of 5.6% and calculating the number of years needed to accumulate $300,000 as our plug figure. As we've continually done in previous illustrations, let's summarize the answers to the other four variables. Our couple is beginning this project with $5,000, seeking to accumulate $300,000 for their daughter's college education. They will contribute $18,000 per year toward the project, and they anticipate being able to earn an average annual rate of return of 5.6% on their invested cash.

Again, using either a software package or a business calculator, we will compute the remaining plug figure, the number of years it will take to build a $300,000 nest egg. Based on the four variables given, the answer to question 3 is that it will take twelve years to accumulate $300,000.

On the surface, it looks like our couple has a small problem. They wanted to accumulate the full amount of their daughter's college fund by the time she starts college, nine years down the road. Since it looks like it will take twelve years, our couple will have to be flexible and make some adjustments in the implementation of their plan. One thing they will not do is make their daughter wait three extra years before she starts her college education.

I'm going to offer a solution that will hopefully keep this illustration straightforward and understandable. I will do this in two steps. First, we will compute how much the couple can accumulate in the nine years before their daughter begins college. Assuming they can successfully raise whatever amount that might be, they will have that amount set aside after nine years to be used to start her college education.

As our second step, we will then compute the amount of time it will take to accumulate the remaining amount to reach the total of $300,000.

Beginning with step one, our couple started with $5,000, and will contribute $18,000 per year for the next nine years. Their contributions will earn an average compounded rate of return of 5.6%. Based on those variables, we calculate that our couple will accumulate approximately $210,000 in nine years when their daughter enters college. To deal with a rounded number, let's assume the couple will set aside $200,000 from what they hope to accumulate in nine years, and they will use the excess $10,000 to begin accumulating the balance they will need to have a total of $300,000.

Coincidentally, the $200,000 they will be setting aside is the projected amount the couple will need to fund the first four years of their daughter's college education.

Now for step two. Again, we summarize the answers to four of the variables that we will know at the end of step one, nine-year period. Our couple will start with $10,000 remaining from the previous accumulation, and contribute the consistent $18,000 per year. The accumulated money will grow, we hope, at an average compounded annual rate of return of 5.6%, and the target amount of accumulation is a nest egg of $100,000.

As we have done throughout these examples, the fifth variable that we will calculate as our plug figure is the number of years it will take to accumulate $100,000. Using our calculator or software package, the number of years it will take is computed to be five years.

Does this additional period of five years present any problems for our couple in the implementation of their plan to provide for their daughter's college education, and potential graduate school? I don't think so.

Remember that at the time our couple completes their first project of accumulating a down payment for their house, their daughter is nine years old. The girl will be eighteen years old nine years later, and hopefully, begin her college studies. Five years after that, at which time our couple will have completed the accumulation of the full $300,000 they were seeking, a total of fourteen years will have passed since beginning their college savings project.

If their daughter finishes undergraduate studies in the typical four years, and if she decides to attend graduate or professional school, she will only have completed one year of her graduate school studies. The completion of the accumulation of the targeted $300,000, with one year remaining of the six total years projected by our couple for their daughter's college fund, will provide the funding for that projected sixth year of college studies.

What has not been discussed, in treating this second financial project separately from the others, is that the daughter will be spending the already accumulated amounts of her college nest egg at the assumed rate of $50,000 per year. Without detailing all the amounts spent, and all the amounts still available to invest and grow at a compounded annual rate, is that by the end of the fifth year of the college education period there is still money left to invest and grow at a compounded rate. When the annual contribution of $18,000 is added to the amount not yet spent by the sixth year of the project, there will be exactly $50,000 remaining to pay for their daughter's final year of the project.

Now let's consider the third and final project of our couple's financial plan, building a retirement nest egg.

Accumulating a Retirement Nest Egg

At this point in the process of implementing a financial plan, after two of the three projects have been completed, a total of seventeen years have gone by. Our couple spent three years accumulating a down payment for the purchase of their first home, and it required fourteen years to accumulate the full amount to fund the potential undergraduate and graduate studies for their daughter's higher education.

Our couple began their three-part financial plan when they were both age thirty (which was seventeen years ago), and they plan to retire at age sixty-five. They will both be sixty-five years old in eighteen years, and that will be the end of the thirty-five-year financial plan, with three separate projects.

As a reminder, their entire financial plan was a combined total of $2.0 million, for which they planned to save and invest. Of that amount, the first $100,000 was for a down payment, and the next $300,000 was for their daughter's higher education pursuits. The first two projects, when added together, total $400,000. With those two projects now completed there remains a balance of $1.6 they wish to accumulate over the final eighteen years until they reach age sixty-five, to supplement other amounts they will receive from Social Security and employer-sponsored retirement plans when they retire.

Let's ask for the final time in this illustration our five basic questions for the accumulation of their desired supplemental retirement fund.

Question 1: How much money does the couple have to begin saving toward their retirement nest egg?

Answer: In the real world, there is a reasonable chance that there might be some money left over from spending for our couple's second financial goal (college education for their daughter), which they would apply toward the accumulation of the third financial goal (retirement). In this illustration, we will assume that our couple spent the entire $300,000 nest egg targeted for their daughter's college education. Thus, the answer to this question is zero, meaning that our couple must now start their saving and investing from scratch.

Question 2: We know that our couple wishes to accumulate

$1.6 million to supplement any retirement income they will receive from Social Security and their respective employers' retirement plans.

Question 3: As discussed above, we know that our couple's goal is to retire at sixty-five. That leaves them with eighteen years to accumulate a nest egg. We will continue with the formula to see how realistic this is.

Question 4: As with the entire overall plan, our couple will continue to contribute $18,000 per year, at the rate of $1,500 per month, for this third project, as they did for the prior two projects.

Question 5: As with the other two financial goals within this plan, the couple is relying on a rate of return percentage of 5.6%.

As I have commented several times in this book, it is important for investors to know and understand which variables they can and cannot control. The key variable we know they cannot control is the economy and the stock market. Thus, it is important that investors choose the desired rate of return on their investment that is realistic for them to achieve, based on historical averages. I feel that 5.6% is one that is realistic and achievable during most market conditions and most economic times—especially over a long period of time.

As a final comment on this third project, accumulation of a retirement nest egg, I want to remind readers that there is one more phase to the retirement portion of this illustration. In reality—once retirement begins and assuming the nest egg is $1.6 million when our couple reaches age sixty-five—the withdrawal or spending phase will begin, and continue through the remainder of their lives, which will end at the time whoever dies second.

So let's run the numbers and revisit question 3 to see how close our couple can come to their eighteen-year goal. As we approach the end of this section of the book, I want to address the revisiting of question 3 by reinforcing the major lesson we all want to learn, and need to learn. If you want to save and invest toward realistic financial goals successfully, it is important to know and understand what you can control, what you can modify, and what you cannot control and must deal with as it is. Once this lesson is learned and assimilated, the less anxiety and stress you will have during the saving and investing process. As we have now repeated numerous times, there are five variables that are dealt with when planning and implementing the growth of a fund of money with which to achieve your financial goals. We have continually asked five questions, the answers to which identify the five variables.

The point I am trying to emphasize is that all is not lost when one or more of the variables are answered in a way not expected or hoped for. In many situations, one or more of the other variables can be modified to make the financial plan workable and successful. The reason other variables can be modified is that you might find that it is one of the other variables that are subject to what you can control.

Now let's address the answer to question 3 and find out whether this requires modification, or if the answer we calculate is something that works for our couple.

To review the other four variables, our couple has just finished planning and implementing the first two projects of the three financial goals they had set out to achieve seventeen years ago. There are now eighteen years left before they hope to retire. A supplemental retirement fund, over and above Social Security and employee retirement plan benefits, is what they seek to achieve.

They are beginning this third project with no funds, but they plan to contribute $18,000 per year during the accumulation process, and they hope to grow a fund to the sum of $1.6 million. They anticipate that all amounts they save up can grow at the average compounded rate of return of 5.6% per year. We now compute the answer to question 3, which asks how many years it will take to reach their financial goal.

Once again, using a business calculator or software program that computes present dollar values, we calculate the answer to be thirty-three years. This means it will take almost twice as long as they would like to accumulate $1.6 million if they contribute only $18,000 per year, and earn a rate of return of only 5.6%.

If you were this couple, you would logically conclude that this plan would not satisfy your needs or wants. So, we ask the questions, what can they change among the variables they can control? Let's revisit all the questions to see if we can get better results.

Question 1 asks how much they have to begin this third project. Let's assume they cannot change that. They cannot change or control the fact that all their funds were used up at the end of the second project, providing their daughter her college education. So the starting amount remains zero.

Question 2 asks how much money they wish to accumulate as a supplemental retirement fund. The number the couple came up with was $1.6 million. They have sufficient control over the selection of this projected number, so they can modify it downward (or even upward) if they wish. But will that satisfy them? The primary reason for going through this entire exercise is to give you the opportunity to accumulate nest eggs of whichever size you choose. If the only answer we can offer, when the numbers are not entirely favorable, is that you have to lower your target expectations, then we might as well just say: save as much as you can at whatever rate of return you can get, and whatever it ends up being is what you have to live with. However, that is not our position. People can achieve their target expectations.

For now, let's stick to the discipline. Our couple wants to accumulate $1.6 million. Let's leave that number unchanged, because that number was the reason for the plan, and it was well thought out when it was chosen.

Question 3 asks how many years the process would take. Based on the answers to all the other questions, the variables we used gave us an answer to question 3 that is beyond our control. The answer of thirty-three years is not a number that our couple wants to hear, or that can make this financial plan work. Since question 3 is the calculated plug figure, the only way we can get that number to change and get smaller is to change one or more of the other variables. So let's move on.

Question 4 asks how much our couple will contribute toward their supplemental retirement fund each year. The answer they have been giving during the first two stages has been $18,000 per year (at the rate of $1,500 per month). I think there is room to modify this variable. After having completed the first two projects, the only financial goal left in this illustration is the saving and investing toward a retirement fund. Some things have changed since beginning their overall financial plan seventeen years ago. If both spouses still maintain their earlier professional careers, it might be realistic to assume they both earn more money than they used to. Also, they are no longer putting a daughter through college. It might be fair to conclude that our couple can control the fact that maybe they can increase their annual contributions toward achieving this third financial goal.

For purposes of modifying their answer to question 4, and hopefully keep to a realistic level the number of years it will take to accumulate $1.6 million, let's assume our couple is willing to substantially increase the amount they will contribute each year, to the sum of $2,500 per month ($30,000 per year). So, the modified answer to question 4 becomes $30,000 per year.

Question 5 asks what average compounded annual rate of return must the invested funds earn to be able to grow to the desired targeted amount. Throughout the various stages of this three-part project, we have used the rate of 5.6% as the rate of compounded growth the invested funds will achieve. We have observed that such a rate of return is realistic and sufficiently modest, over the long term, so as to be historically justified, assuming our couple makes investments into the traditional stock market.

Maybe the best approach at this point is to make the answer to question 5 become the calculated plug figure. The rate of return number may have to be increased in any event, because we are trying to create a realistic financial plan for our couple to implement. Let's go back and ask our couple to select an answer to question 3, the number of years this project will take, to see if we can then calculate a realistic and achievable rate of return as the answer to question 5.

Revisiting question 3, which asks how many years it will take to accumulate $1.6 million as a supplemental retirement fund, let's see if our couple finds this variable within their ability to control.

When we first addressed this three-part project, our couple was thirty years old, wanted to buy a house, send their daughter to college, and save for retirement at age sixty-five. Age sixty-five seemed a long way off. Now, seventeen years later, views toward retirement age have broadened a bit. Maybe our couple has changed their view, and working longer than age sixty-five might not seem to be a major obstacle. In the alternative, one spouse might continue to work after age sixty-five, and the other might choose to retire at that age. No matter how they address this issue, it is conceivable that they would be willing to take some extra years to be able to amass the next egg amount they seek to achieve.

To make this illustration appear as realistic as possible, let's assume our couple is willing to extend the number of years to complete this third project by four years. In other words, the answer to this final revisited question 3 is now going to be twenty-two years. The couple will wait for retirement until age sixty-nine, or if one of them retires earlier than that, they will continue to make annual contributions and grow their nest egg fund until they reach age sixty-nine.

Now we do a final revisit to answer question 5, the average annual rate of return their investments will require. Summarizing the facts for one final time, the couple will start with zero funds, but will contribute $30,000 annually for a period of twenty-two years toward a target nest egg of $1.6 million to supplement their retirement income. Calculating the answer to question 5 in the usual way, we compute the average compounded rate of return their invested savings needs to earn will be approximately 7.7% annually.

Although this newly computed rate of return is a couple of percentage points higher than the 5.6% we had been using for the first two projects, I am pleased to say that this new percentage is still a realistic and achievable percentage. Based on historical rates of return for the general stock market over the last eighty to one hundred years, it is well below what the long-term compounded averages have been.

Nothing is guaranteed in the world of stock investing, but in the exercise of financial planning and implementation, when the desired rate of return is well below historical averages, it should help reduce the stress and anxiety of the financial planning process.

This section of the book was very detailed and specific as to answering five key questions and identifying the variables necessary for creation and implementation of any financial plan. If you are going to be serious and disciplined about achieving your financial goals, you have to do something more than just saying to yourself, "I've got to start saving for my financial future." You have to know what you can and cannot control.

More importantly, the overwhelming message stressed in this book is that you have the ability to create and implement a plan to achieve your goals without stress, anxiety, and fear. This does not mean the process automatically takes care of itself. You have to work hard at being habitual and disciplined. You have to select the right kind of advisers or support people to help keep you on your straight path. But it is not magic, and does not require good luck to be successful. Of course, it works better if you don't run into a heavy dosage of bad luck. But luck (good and bad) has very little to do with successful planning implementation.

Planning and implementing your future goals requires you to know the answers to five key questions, understanding what you can and cannot control, understanding the tools you have at your disposal, and recognizing the land mines to avoid.

This section deals with financial planning. The reason this section is different from every other financial planning program you've ever encountered is because of its simplicity and flexibility. You don't need to fill out a lengthy questionnaire or have a boring meeting with a professional adviser to get a relatively clear picture of where you are now and where you need to get to in order to achieve your financial goals. In this section, there are five key questions that should be asked and answered to implement your financial plan. The five questions are as follows:

1. How much money do you need to accumulate to achieve your financial goal?

2. How much money do you have now to begin the implementation of your plan?

3. How many years do you expect it will take to accumulate the desired amount?

4. How much new money will you contribute to your plan on a regular basis?

5. What annual compounded rate of return, on average, will be needed to accumulate the amount you desire?

As was explained in this section, you must supply the answers to any four questions, and the answer to the fifth question is derived by a mathematical computation, meaning it is a plug figure.

In most situations, the plug figure is the answer to question 5, the desired rate of return, but that is not always the case. Any one of the five questions can be left unanswered and be treated as the plug figure. It will be computed with the answers you supply for the other four questions.

A business calculator or common software program can compute the answer to whichever is chosen as the plug figure, after answering any four of the five key questions. A calculator link is supplied on my website, customizewallstreet.com, which will help you to readily solve the plug figure from the answers to whichever four questions you choose to supply.

Several illustrations were presented in this section to give a cross section of scenarios that could apply to almost any person or family seeking to save and invest in the effort to realize their financial goal. These examples were for saving to buy a car, for growing a college fund, for accumulating a retirement fund (two illustrations were presented), and finally, for a combination of financial goals. It doesn't matter if you are saving for one financial goal or for a series or combination of financial goals; the financial planning process is the same. The discipline required is the same. The five key questions you must ask and answer are the same.

The five key questions are not only asked and answered for the period when the fund is being accumulated, but an additional set of five key questions need be asked and answered for the period in your life when you are spending the funds you have accumulated. These years are referred to as the spending years. In some instances, the spending period is all in one lump sum, like buying a car, buying a house, or paying for a child's wedding. However, in most situations, such as retirement, the spending period might last for as many years as the accumulation period.

The five key questions for the spending period are slightly different than those for the accumulation period, and are as follows:

1. How much money have you accumulated that is now available for withdrawal?

2. How much money do you want or need to withdraw each period (weekly, monthly, quarterly)?

3. How much time (months, years, decades) do you expect to be taking regular withdrawals?

4. How much money do you expect or want to have left, if any, at the end of the withdrawal period (months, years, life expectancy) to leave to heirs or apply to another financial purpose?

5. What annual rate of return (compounded) will you need to maintain on average during the withdrawal period to achieve your goal?

Obviously, if the financial goal involves spending for a one-time project (purchase of a car, house, vacation, or paying for a wedding), the question related to the number of years of withdrawal will have a single-digit response. All the other questions will be answered similarly to the five questions asked for the accumulation period. One of the five questions will be a plug figure using either a business calculator or a software program designed to compute present dollar values. In most cases, the plug figure will be the desired annual rate of return needed to achieve the investor's financial goal. But the plug figure can be the answer to any of the five questions, as long as you have answers to the other four.

In the case of a saver-investor who has multiple financial goals, the most straightforward method for implementation would be to handle each of the goals separately, as if each of them is the only goal.

However, you might need to implement each goal during the same time frame so implement them individually to the best of your ability.

A final point in summarizing this section is to emphasize the need for discipline and consistency when seeking to achieve your financial goals. If, for example, your plan indicates you should contribute $200 every month to achieve your goal, then you must continuously and consistently contribute $200 every single month. If you miss your contribution just one time, then it takes a contribution of $400 the next time to keep up. If you miss it twice, then you need to contribute $600 to make up for the missed payments. If this pattern of missed payments should continue, your financial plan will quickly fall apart. The payment required to catch up might become so overwhelming, the probability of achieving your goal could become minuscule.

Financial planning need not be confusing or complex. I hope all readers recognize that discipline and consistency are traits that are substantially within your control, and are not dependent on the state of the economy or the direction of the stock market.

SECTION 4:

PUTTING IT ALL TOGETHER

We have traveled a long road. We've brought a better understanding of Wall Street by identifying the distractions and misconceptions it throws our way, as well as the favorable tools it offers any of us who choose to use them. We've discussed not only the importance of identifying your financial goals and the methods for doing so, but took it one step further by laying out concrete steps for reaching those goals. Each step along the way has been intended to educate and empower you; to demonstrate the tools and resources you have before you; to be transparent in presenting what you can and cannot control. To reach our destination, we still have a short way to go to get where we want to be. In this last section, we will do our best to put it all together.

In this final section, I will continue to stress the importance of one of the main themes of this book. No one can expect to consistently—and with a high probability of success—achieve their financial goals unless the element of saving and continuous contributions is added to the investment process. It is the process of continuous contributions that offsets, more than any other activity, the impact and stress of up and down stock market prices. It is the element of saving and the type of investing that is totally within the control of the investor.

Clearly, the main purpose and premise of this book is to provide readers with methods to reduce stress and worry in the effort to be a successful investor, and to successfully achieve your financial aspirations.

Now that we have a better understanding of some of the kinds of distractions we should try to avoid, and the focus required to select and implement financial goals, how do we find and select investment vehicles that will get us where we want to be? We learned in the second section of this book about the ten powerful investment tools that will help us grow a nest egg with less stress and worry, but we now face the question of which investment vehicles will best employ the powerful tools we want to work for us. Let's approach this by looking at a series of questions we should be able to address sequentially.

The first question you should ask yourself is, "What are my financial goals?" We've already looked at a variety of examples in Section 3. Your situation might be similar to the ones presented in that section, or they might be totally different. Whether they are similar or different, the approach and the process is the same. The five key questions apply in virtually all situations, and are adaptable to whatever your personal situation might be.

The second question you should ask is, "Am I implementing my financial plan in a productive and disciplined manner?" This involves saving and investing in a consistent manner and gradually building your desired nest egg to fund your financial goals.

The third question you should ask is, "Am I achieving an average compounded rate of return on my investments that is consistent with achieving the desired growth of my nest egg?"

As you address these questions, there is an additional point to keep in mind. Many financial books might leave you with the impression that the only successful investment is going to be the investments recommended by the author. In my opinion, if an author pushes one type of investment as being superior to others, it could be an indication that he or she has an agenda or ulterior motive to promote such investments. I assure you that is not the case with this book. I feel that the best investment for any individual investor, not a speculator, is one that the individual is comfortable with, knowledgeable about, and has confidence in. That particular investment may not be the one the author is most familiar with, but is potentially just as effective, all the same.

Naturally, as a professional portfolio manager, I have my favorite investments, those with which I am most familiar, enjoy, and have found success. However, you will note a lack of any reference to these investments throughout this book. I have no intention of urging my readers to necessarily select my preferences. I choose investments for my saving and investing program that are comfortable and successful for me. I feel certain that the same can be said of most other people with a long track record of successful investing.

Understanding that each person should select investment categories that work best for them, it is also a good idea to have more than one category of investments. You are free to own stocks and real estate, for example. You might choose to own gold, while at the same time also be invested in conservative municipal bonds.

There is nothing in this book intended to suggest that you should pick only one style of investing, or put all your eggs in one basket. That would not be a wise thing to do.

My purpose in this wrap-up section of the book is to introduce some brief commentary on a variety of investment types that will hopefully serve the purpose of educating and exposing you to options that can help you achieve your financial goals. The list of investment types I will present is by no means exhaustive. If you don't like the kinds of investments I introduce, there are plenty more from which to choose. If you come across an investment category not mentioned in this book, you are certainly welcome to go to my website and send me a message or e-mail to ask questions about a category with which you are not familiar.

Let's now have a brief look at some of the more common saving and investment categories, and methods of holding your savings and investments that are available to everyday folks seeking to grow a financial nest egg.

Types of Accounts & Methods of Holding Assests

The Cookie Jar / Under the Mattress

Money in a cookie jar simply means that you have it stashed somewhere nonconventional, but hidden and safe. This could be a cookie jar, your freezer, under your mattress, etc. It means, very simply, that you are saving without the benefit of investing. It means that while you may be diligent in making continuous contributions to the hidden nest egg, the value of each dollar you set aside is decreasing at the rate of inflation because you are not implementing any tools to make your money grow. As such, you are using none of the ten powerful tools. While your money is incredibly liquid, this category is ill suited for reaching any significant financial goals unless you can put so much money aside on a regular basis that it negates the need to make that money grow through investment. However, if this were that case, even the most conservative and safe investment options such as a savings account or CDs would make more sense than simply letting the money sit.

In addition to putting money under the mattress or in the cookie jar, there are several other places that folks traditionally park their savings dollars that fall in the same category. These other places for parking or holding their case for safekeeping include safe-deposit boxes, gold, artwork, and precious stones.

A safe-deposit box can hold your cash or legal documents like deeds and wills. Once placed in the box, the cash cannot earn interest and loses the opportunity to compound and grow.

Similarly, precious stones, gold, and artwork themselves do not pay interest or dividends, so they are viewed as just being held until they go up in value. This is true whether they are stored in a vault or displayed in one's home. As far as their monetary worth, they are more like speculation than investment.

Now then, if someone rents out their art collection, then that would be a form of an investment, because the rent represents cash being generated by the asset in question.

Brokerage Accounts / Bank Accounts

If a person wishes to hold stocks, mutual funds, bonds, CDs, savings accounts, checking accounts, or even commodities and options, it will require the opening of an account at a recognized brokerage firm, bank, or credit union. This will be the institution that has the custody of your investment assets. This does not mean the institution is the owner of your assets. Assuming the institution you choose is fully registered and regulated by a federal or state agency, these are traditionally the safest places to park your investments. They provide ready access to your holdings and provide good recordkeeping of what you have placed there and what you have withdrawn from your accounts.

Even if such an institution were to run itself into financial difficulty—to the extent they have custody of their customers' assets—government regulators would treat such holdings as being held "in trust," and would not expose these customer assets to the claims of general creditors of the institution.

Various Types of Retirement Accounts: 401(k)s, IRAs, and Pensions

Many people confuse their retirement plans, whether set up on their own or provided by their employers, with the types of investments they choose. Someone will comment at a cocktail party, or to a neighbor, that their 401(k) went down by 30% last year, for example. They might comment on their IRA savings plan as if it were an investment category itself. This is a point of confusion for a lot of folks.

Any saving and investment plan is not an investment itself; it is a type of an account in which you can select one or more types of investments. A college savings plan, one that might have some tax benefits, for example, is a type of account that certain legislation has given favored tax treatment. The same is true with several types of retirement accounts, such as SEP-IRA, Roth IRA, traditional IRA, 401(k) plan, and defined contribution plan. Defining and explaining the details of these various types of tax favored accounts or plans are beyond the scope of this book. Suffice to say, each of these types of accounts generally receives favored tax treatment by the IRS. They are sometimes referred to collectively as "qualified" plans or accounts. The means that investments or savings held in these types of accounts are "qualified" to receive favored tax treatment.

For purposes of understanding and implementing your financial planning goals, readers should be aware that these types of retirement accounts may be opened at any bank, brokerage firm, credit union, or mutual fund company.

An investor must still decide what investments to make within these types of qualified retirement accounts.

Trusts / Estates

Like qualified retirement accounts discussed above, a person may be a beneficiary, trustee, executor, or administrator of an estate, or might be designated as such in someone's will or living trust.

A probate estate or living trust in and of itself is not a type of investment. In actuality, a trust or probate estate is a form of legal title to an entity designed to pass assets from one generation to another, and is designed to be a temporary entity (many of which can last for years) that lasts as long as it takes to complete the transfer of assets.

Even though they may only be temporary in length, trusts and estates are not only permitted, but in many cases, they are mandated to make investments. In such cases, the trustee or executor is technically the legal owner of the investments, in the name of the trust or the estate, for the benefit of the heirs or beneficiaries.

The trustee or executor will have to make all the same investment decisions and selections as would an individual seeking to save and invest for the future. The only limitation when dealing with investments for trusts or estates is the caution to be more conscious of not exposing the invested assets to excessive risk.

Fee-Based Registered Investment Advisory Firms

Investors who use registered investment advisor (RIA) firms are usually looking for two things. They are seeking professional investment advice, and they want an advisor who has an incentive to improve their investment results. These firms take a unique perspective from that of a typical stock brokerage firm. Most RIA firms charge fees based on the dollar amount of assets they are managing, rather than charging commissions on trades. A typical percentage rate is 1% per year of the average total assets being managed by the advisory firm. If a RIA firm increases your assets, they earn their percentage on a larger amount. Thus, their focus is on increasing your assets, not making multiple trades.

Types of Investments

As we look closely at the various examples presented in the previous section, let's ask this question: How successful can you be as an investor, using the tools Wall Street provides, to earn the required rates of return to meet your financial goals? The answer depends on the relative success you have in achieving the average compounded rate of return your financial plan requires.

It's important for us to always be as realistic as we can be when it comes to the average rates of return that we need to achieve over a several-year period. As I've stressed many times in this book, beating a benchmark rate of return is not the measure of success. Sustaining the average rate of return required by your financial plan is the measure of success. What is that number in the real world?

If we review the examples from the previous section, I think it will show that in a majority of the situations, an average compounded rate of return ranging from about 5% annually to a high of about 7.5% annually covered most of the examples. Which types of investments can yield those levels of returns over a multi-year period?

Regulatory restrictions, and just plain ethics, prohibit a financial advisor or a portfolio manager from promising any particular rates of return by using investment products of Wall Street. I subscribe to the wisdom of those restrictions, so you won't find any promises in this book.

With that said, it seems appropriate for me to identify for readers those types of investments that have historically delivered certain average rates of return. Likewise, as one learns how various investments work, and the kind of cash flows they deliver, I feel justified in discussing the math related to such investments. If the resulting cash flows are calculated against the dollars invested, conclusions can be made as to what the expected average rate of return might be. These can be done using basic business calculations.

Real Estate

For many of us, our first home purchase represents both the first major investment we make as well as perhaps the culmination of the first major financial goal we have accomplished by saving up for a down payment. Regardless of how you have come to own your first home, it is important to recognize that it is an investment. Each month that you pay down the principal balance of your mortgage, you are in essence putting that money into savings. Like any investment, there is certainly a risk. In this case, it is that your property value will maintain or increase. But even if it does not, by the time you pay off your mortgage you have eliminated a major living expense (a mortgage) for the rest of your life. The investment category of real estate includes rental properties, land ownership, house flipping, etc.

In most cases, investments in real estate involve certain risks or obstacles that many folks feel are too much of a burden to overcome. The capital costs, meaning the dollars needed to invest, are generally much larger than investments in typical IRA accounts or 401(k) plans at work. In most cases, real estate requires financing packages with lenders assessing your line of credit to be able to invest. During good economic times, the risk of loss with real estate is often less than more volatile investments, such as the stock market, but there is a much longer time factor involved in the exercise of buying and selling real estate. This is called liquidity risk, meaning that if one day you want to sell off your real estate investment, it might take many weeks, or months, or even years to sell, depending on economic conditions and potential demand for the property being sold.

On the plus side, since most real estate ownership is entered into for the long term, meaning several years, most real estate investments increase in value over time. We all know that real estate can decrease in value, as was the case during the four-

or five-year period preceding the writing of this book. But the historical pattern with real estate investing is an upward trend in the value of land, and an upward trend in rents charged by property owners.

If a person with smaller amounts of saved dollars wishes to invest in real estate, there are ways to do that as well, but usually, that will be in the form of shared ownership. There are limited partnerships and stock offerings known as real estate investment trusts, to name just a few. A detailed explanation and discussion of such investments are beyond the scope of this book. I recommend to my readers that any Internet search engine or real estate professional can help you get started with such investments.

The good news is that with real estate investing, assuming you're collect rents from leasing investment property, you are taking advantage of many of the powerful tools of investing. Compounding, time, discipline, limited leverage, limited hedging, growing revenues and earnings, just to name a few, are indeed some of the powerful tools that come into play with successful real estate investments.

Stock Investments

Stock investments are probably the most common type of investments known on Wall Street. As we've already pointed out, the New York Stock Exchange, the American Stock Exchange, and the NASDAQ exchange are the heart and center of what we know as Wall Street. We've spent a good portion of this book analyzing Wall Street, critiquing Wall Street, and deciphering Wall Street. Even with all this poking and pulling, we've still managed to applaud Wall Street as providing some of the finest investment tools available to American savers and investors. Those tools focus on investments in fine American companies through the form of buying and selling stock in such fundamentally sound companies.

Let's briefly revisit some points made earlier in the book. It is important to recall the difference between investing and speculating. It would be the purchasing of stocks as investments—especially those paying consistent dividends—that we would endorse as a category of investments capable of helping readers attain their financial goals. Stocks purchased and sold for speculative purposes is an exercise in gambling, not unlike going to a casino or purchasing lottery tickets. It is true that you can make a great deal of money speculating in stocks, but it is not ideal as a consistent investment program designed to help savers make investments for achieving their long-term financial goals.

Ideally, stock investments in companies paying consistent dividends, including companies who periodically increase their dividends, are particularly suited for implementation of your financial plan for building a nest egg for the future. For example, if the initial investment into a stock pays a 3.5% dividend, and the company grows the dividend payment by 10% per year, then after five years the percentage yield grows into just a little more than 5.6%, based on the original cost of the investment. This increase in dividend yield will occur whether or not the stock price grows or decreases during the five-year period. If the stock price does grow over five years, the total return on this investment increases even more; when adding in the gain in price, it grows even more.

The beauty of stock investing, especially those involving dividend-paying stocks, is that stock values usually increase over time at least at the rate of inflation. This occurrence is not absolute in all cases, but often appears to be the trend. Even with modest stock price increases, growth in dividend payments will usually increase the percentage return for such stock investments.

Long-term stock investing can be a wonderful tool to combat the effects of inflation, as well as for growing your financial nest egg. The historical returns on investments in mainstream stocks are usually favorable over the long term. Naturally, the classic warning applies regarding all stock investments, that past performance is no guarantee of similar future rates of return from such investments. Historically, the evidence supports successful rates of return on stock investing. If we look at recent performance over the last few decades, the compounded annualized rate return of the popular S&P 500 Index, from 1962 through 2011, averaged approximately 10.6% per year. Several years during that period had extremely wide fluctuations, in some years down more than 20% and some years up to more than 20%, but on average over the entire period, investments grew on average at a compounded rate higher than most financial plans required. As a point of reference, this documented average rate of return far exceeded the rate required by any of the various illustrations presented in Section 3 of this book.

On a historical basis, the kinds of returns required by common financial plans have been achieved in the past by investments in the general stock market, as measured by the standardized S&P 500 benchmark index.

Bonds / Fixed Income Investments

Most investors think of bond investing as being very conservative. Yet there is a comfort in most bond investments of knowing that interest payments are going to be paid no matter what. There are bond programs that contain a potential for risk of loss, but that is not the usual case.

Bonds are usually long-term investments, ranging in maturity from twenty years to thirty years. Most bonds are issued by corporations, and they usually pay interest on regular intervals, at least once a year, or more frequently. Interest rates paid on bond investments vary, depending on the riskiness of the bond investment. The longer the number of years before a bond matures, the higher the interest rate will usually be.

Bonds issued by the US federal government are the safest category of bonds. Those that have longer maturity are referred to as treasury bonds (frequently twenty years or thirty years until maturity), and those of shorter duration are referred to as treasury bills (usually ten years or less until maturity).

Once again, if we look at the performance of treasuries over the last few decades, the compounded annualized rate return of long-term treasury bonds, from 1962 through 2011, averaged approximately 7.24% per year. The compounded annualized rate of return of the shorter duration treasury bills, from 1962 through 2011, averaged approximately 5.22% per year.

Once again, it is appropriate to state that past performance does not guarantee the same results in the future. Historical evidence supports the proposition that on a long-term basis, those financial plans that require rates of return ranging from 5% to 7% (on average over a period of years) have been achieved in the past with some of the safest investments available to all of us— US treasuries.

In addition to the federal government, other public entities also offer fixed-income investments. The most common of these types are referred to as municipal bonds. These are issued by different state and local governments like counties, cities, school districts, and water districts. Most bond issues in this category pay interest that is federal government tax-free, and sometimes even state government tax-free. With the tax-free nature of their interest payments, the interest rates are lower than that of most corporate bonds.

In addition to bonds, there are a couple of types of stock investments that are similar to bonds because they resemble fixed-income instruments by paying higher dividends than general common stocks. These other types are preferred stock and real estate investment trust (REITS). Preferred stock is a corporate stock that usually pays higher rates of dividends than common stock, and the dividend payments have preference ahead of the corporation's ordinary dividends. The regular or ordinary dividends of a corporation are generally not paid out until preferred dividends are paid first to the shareholders. If there is not enough money to pay all dividends declared by a corporation, the preferred dividends are paid first. In other words, they are treated more like a debt or bond obligation than a corporation's ordinary common stock dividends. In addition, the dividend rates on preferred stock are usually higher than the rates for ordinary common stock dividends. With the higher dividend rates, the stock prices of preferred stock tend to be more stable than the prices of common stock. The price stability ends up holding the percentage yield on preferred stock close to the stated percentage. Again, this is similar to the interest percentages declared on bond investments.

REITS are also stock investments that have characteristics similar to bonds. A REIT is usually a conglomerate of real property holdings that usually collect rents from tenants for a host of income properties, some residential, others commercial, including office complexes and resort properties. These entities then distribute the vast majority of their net rental income to the REIT shareholders, in the form of dividends. These dividends are computed after deducting all the expenses of operating and maintaining the various properties.

The dividend payments from REIT stocks are similar to that of preferred stock in the sense that the dividend percentages are often higher than that of ordinary common stock, and as such have similarity to interest payments on bonds. Dividend payments of REITS might vary a bit more than bonds or preferred stock, since they are subject to economic conditions related to real estate. Excessive rental vacancies can affect revenues and cash flows, and thereby put dividend payments at risk. Under normal economic conditions, rental revenues and subsequent dividend payouts can be quite steady from ownership of REIT stocks.

As a final subcategory of fixed-income investments, there are high-yield bonds. These types of bonds are typical corporate-debt instruments, but the rate of interest on such bonds is generally higher than the rates of corporate investment-grade bonds, and higher than US Treasury debt instruments.

The reason that some corporate bonds are referred to as "high yield" is that the corporations in question are not as strong financially as the major corporations with fundamentally solid financial statements. For weaker corporations to attract investors to put money into their debt instruments, they have to offer higher interest rates on their bonds. There is a greater risk of default with such bonds, so the higher interest payments are compensation for the higher risk. The interest rates on high-yield bonds are often similar to those of REITS and preferred stock.

One interesting observation about high-yield bonds is that their price performance often resembles the price fluctuations of the common stock in the same companies. The value of the common stock and the high-yield bonds can be a reflection of the general risk of investing in corporate businesses. Since these types of companies are viewed as riskier than the big industry leaders, both the common stock and the high-yield bonds can return excessive profits, or excessive risk of loss.

In summary, depending on economic conditions, there are many fixed income and bond investment choices that have the potential of delivering rates of return required by your financial plan.

Life Insurance / Annuities

Many people don't know that most, but not all, life insurance policies have investment features. They are frequently sold by insurance professionals as investments. Annuity policies are more commonly known as investment vehicles, and usually sold as such by annuity professionals. The key difference between life insurance and annuities is how they are viewed by the individuals who purchase them. Life insurance policies are viewed primarily as providing death benefits to people who survive the insured person. Annuities are viewed primarily as providing living benefits to the person who purchases them after a certain number of years go by.

The investment portion of either a life insurance policy or an annuity policy relates to the type of funding that provides the source of payment of the proceeds to the policy beneficiaries.

Whether it is a death benefit policy (life insurance) or a life benefit policy (annuity), insurance companies that offer such policies receive the premium payments from policyholders as payment for the policies. Then the companies build up cash values to be able to eventually pay out the benefits required by the policies. Policy benefits are paid out at death for life insurance, and after a designated number of years for annuities.

Here's where the investment comes in. Several years back, insurance company executives realized that the cash built up from premium payments paid by policy holders could be managed more effectively than it had been. The companies are required to keep sufficient reserves of cash to pay benefits to policyholders, but amounts in excess of the required reserves can be invested in growing even more cash. Traditionally, such cash was invested in fixed-income investments, like treasury bonds and bills. With changes related to insurance regulations, products were created where each policyholder could choose whether to invest cash designated for their benefit payments in the traditional safe treasuries, or they could now be invested in various mutual funds to take advantage of stock market gains.

This is now true for both "variable" life insurance and "variable" annuities. The term variable implies that the outcome of the chosen investments can vary with the success of the stock market. So, savers and investors can now consider using either variable life insurance or variable annuities for building a nest egg to accomplish their financial goals.

All the nuances of variable life insurance and variable annuity policies are beyond the scope of this book. However, these programs now have some minimum "guarantees" that they build into their policies that could make these attractive choices for saving and investing. Caution: you need to be aware that any program that includes built-in guarantees usually comes with higher fees than typical mutual fund investments or typical stock investments. It may be worth it to pay such additional fees if you want the comfort of knowing that your investment will earn a certain minimum percentage even during rough economic conditions.

I have one more comment about guaranteed minimum returns in annuity policies. Any guarantee is only worth as much the ability of the entity giving the guarantee to honor its commitment. If an annuity policy contains a provision for a guaranteed minimum rate of return, and the company issuing the policy becomes insolvent or goes bankrupt, then the guarantee could become pretty much worthless. In the event the company does not have enough assets or enough reserves to cover the guarantees of all of its annuity policyholders, then there is a chance such "guarantees" might not be honored.

As an investment vehicle, life insurance and annuity policies with variable investment features can be excellent vehicles for achieving consistent returns over long periods. I recommend that readers interested in learning more about these investment features consult with a life insurance and annuity specialist for more details. The beauty of some of these programs, especially life insurance, is they can provide benefits for the next generation as well.

Illustrations of Investments Using the Powerful Tools

As you can see, there are numerous types of investments, any of which can be used to implement your financial plan. Some types can take advantage of all ten powerful tools, yet other types might employ only a few. It is beyond the scope of this book to delve into the workings of all types of investment categories, because I'm not necessarily sufficiently equipped to analyze the success all the various investment types. With that said, I readily admit that I'm most familiar with stock market investing as compared to several of the categories I've mentioned. There is one type of investing, of which I am most familiar, that has the potential to employ most or all of the ten powerful tools of investing. As I said earlier, the ten powerful tools are available with many Wall Street investments, and I urge investors to take advantage of them. I repeat: the tools are available to us all.

Covered Call Strategy

One type of investing I often encourage experienced stock investors to learn about is an investment program I've used for many years in my investment accounts, and in many of the portfolios, I manage professionally. The technique I'm suggesting is generally referred to as a "covered call" program. I will illustrate two versions of the covered call program below. In my opinion, at least nine and possibly all ten of the powerful tools come into play in this conservative approach to stock investing.

The illustrations I'm about to present are neither an endorsement nor a recommendation that people should necessarily adopt the type of investments I will present. The purpose is to show you that all or most of the powerful investment tools can be used when making investments on Wall Street. Yes, there are distractions on Wall Street, but the powerful tools are available for all who understand them and wish to use them.

The type of investment I'm now going to present involves

both the buying of stocks and the employment of stock option contracts. Most people refer to this as a "covered call" strategy. I often refer to it as a "conservative covered call" program. No investment style can guarantee absolute safety, and depending on market conditions, some strategies are safer than others. I strongly feel that the way I use a conservative covered call program improves your chances (but there are no guarantees) of meeting the desired compounded rate of return for the successful buildup of your desired nest egg.

To start with, here are the basic elements—the parts and pieces—of the conservative covered call investment strategy that anyone using Wall Street investment tools can implement. All that is required is that you understand how to implement the strategy.

First, you should select a stock you like, to be purchased in 100 share increments. You can buy 100 shares, 500 shares, 3,500 shares, or whatever amount your monetary resources will allow you to purchase. The strategy works nicely if you choose a stock that also pays a regular dividend.

Second, you should designate a target price at which you would be willing to sell that stock. The selected selling price should be chosen in standardized multiples of $10, $5, or $2.50, depending on how high the price is per share. As you will see from the two illustrations, it does not matter if you pick a target-selling price above or below the price you originally paid for the stock. Most people will choose a target price above the price they paid for the stock, because that will express a hope for additional returns from the capital gain.

Third, you will now want to execute the trades properly, which includes buying the desired number of shares of stock (in multiples of 100), while at the same instance, or at some point after buying the shares of stock, you will sell "covered call options" directly related to the stock that you just purchased. Virtually all reputable brokerage firms (including discount firms, online firms, and traditional full-service firms) allow their clients and account holders to execute covered call option transactions. Most firms consider the program conservative enough to all such trading in most qualified retirement accounts, such as IRA accounts, even some 401(k) retirement plan accounts. Since the "call" options are contracts to sell the stock in question at a certain price on or before a certain date, the call options contracts are referred to as derivatives. These call option contracts are "derived" from the underlying shares of stock to which they refer.

Fourth, as a part of the trading process, you should understand the cash flows that are involved. If the stock you decide to purchase costs $50 per share, then each 100 shares requires an investment of $5,000. Transaction fees, commissions, and taxation all definitely exist, but are eliminated from these illustrations to avoid making these examples excessively complex. In addition to paying for the shares, there is cash involved in selling the covered calls. If you, as an investor, have chosen to fix a target price by selling covered call options, the "options exchanges" will have placed a value, meaning a cash premium, which you will get paid for by selling covered calls that lock in a selling price. For example, if you paid $50 per share for the stock, and you're willing to sell the stock if it rises to or exceeds $55 per share by the end of six months from when you bought the stock, the options exchange might award you $3 per share for locking in the selling price of $55 per share for the next six months.

Hopefully, you now get the idea that in a sample transaction, such as the one described in the above paragraph, the investor can earn money in three possible ways: you could: 1) receive $5 per share capital gain if the stock rises above $55 per share; 2) receive cash dividends if it is the stock of a dividend-paying company; and 3) receive $3 per share as option premium if you sell a covered call option contract obligating you to sell the shares at $55 per share on or before the end of the next six months. In summary, you will actually put up less cash to purchase stocks for which you are willing to sell covered calls. In the above example, the investor paid $5,000 for 100 shares of the stock, but immediately received back $300 for each call option contract the investor sold (100 x $3 premium per share). It may not be a lot of money, but the investor is out of pocket on $4,700 instead of $5,000 by selling covered calls.

Fifth, now you watch and wait to see if the price of the stock rises above the target price by the date when the call options expire (in the above example, six months down the road). If the stock price at the end of the six months is even slightly above the $55 target price, it will automatically be sold by the options exchange for $55 per share. For those familiar with covered call options, it is well known that even if the stock price rises substantially above the $55 per share target price, you have made a commitment to sell the shares for $55 per share. Whether the price is slightly above $55 or greatly above $55, it is the exact amount (less transaction costs) you will be paid.

For investors not familiar with stock options contracts generally, and covered call options, in particular, I strongly urge you to consult your trusted broker or advisor to obtain for you all the appropriate explanatory brochures offered by the Options Clearing Corporation (OCC), to familiarize you with the risks of options and covered calls. As mentioned earlier, covered call options are usually recognized as the most conservative of the options trading techniques, but there are certainly risks of loss that investors should be warned about and made to understand.

In-depth explanations and disclosures of the risks of covered call options contracts are beyond the scope of this book. There are numerous publications, books, and workshops available for all those interested in learning more. Feel free to visit my website for additional references to publications and examples of covered call options, references to which are provided in the appendix of this book. Now let's get to the examples.

Illustration #6: Covered Call with Target Selling Price <u>Above</u> Purchase Price

Before going through the two examples, I'd like to mention a particular view I have about the behavior of stock prices over time. My view is more practical than scientific, but it gives me a comforting perspective when making decisions about stock investments. If you invest in a particular stock, and let's assume it's one of the larger well-known American companies, the company has probably issued millions, perhaps even billions of shares that are traded every day on the stock exchanges. You and I, as average investors, have almost no influence on the price fluctuations of that stock over time.

When assessing the chances that I might make a gain from the purchase of any particular stock, I have concluded that over any period of time, whether it is long or short, from the time I purchase the stock until the time I sell the stock there are five possible price movements that the stock might make. The possible price moves the stock might have made by the time I wish to sell are: 1) the price ends up unchanged from the purchase price; 2) the price goes up but just by a small amount; 3) the price goes up by a large amount; 4) the price goes down but just by a small amount; or 5) the price goes down by a large amount.

Depending on the length of time I might own the stock before selling it, the price might make all of five possible moves during the time I own it, but we are only looking at the end result on the day the stock actually gets sold. At the time I eventually sell the stock in question, there will actually be only one of these possible outcomes in comparison to the price I paid for my stock.

For purposes of the two examples I will present, let's assume that the time frame will be short enough that the stock will only make one of these five possible price moves prior to being sold. The illustrations will analyze the outcome with each of the possible price moves, one at a time. The chances or probabilities that any one of these five outcomes will actually occur might be difficult to statistically calculate. For purposes of these illustrations, I will oversimplify the probabilities. Let's assume that each of the five suggested possible outcomes has an equal probability as any of the others. With five possible outcomes, each outcome has a one-fifth or 20% probability of occurring.

In both examples below, I have chosen to illustrate the covered call strategy by using the stock of a real company. I used real price quotes for both the stock and the related call option contracts. The prices presented in the illustrations are those published at the close of the stock market and options markets on the date in question. The stock I chose is the company Occidental Petroleum Corporation, prices for which are usually quoted using the trading symbol OXY. The trading date I chose was June 24, 2013. The hypothetical trade I created for these illustrations was for the purchase of 100 shares of OXY stock, priced at the closing stock market price on that date of $88.65 per share.

In the first illustration, I added the hypothetical sale of one covered call option contract (covering 100 shares of OXY), which then obligated me to sell the 100 shares of OXY that I had just purchased at the target price (often referred to as the "strike" price) of $90 per share, on or before November 15, 2013. In exchange for selling the covered call, and obligating myself to sell 100 shares OXY if stock price exceeds $90 per share at the close of the trading on November 15, 2013, I received a cash "premium" of $5.05 per share for that commitment.

In the second illustration, I likewise bought 100 shares of OXY at the close of trading on June 24, 2013, for the purchase price of $88.65 per share. In this second illustration, I added the hypothetical sale of one covered call option contract (covering 100 shares of OXY), which then obligated me to sell the 100 shares of OXY that I had just purchased. In this case, I obligated myself to a target-selling price (often referred to as the "strike" price) of $85 per share. You will note that in this case, I selected a target-selling price lower than the price I paid for the shares of OXY stock. If the price of OXY finished higher than that price at the close of the market on November 15, 2013, I would be obligated to sell it for $85 per share. In exchange for selling the covered call, and obligating myself to sell 100 shares OXY if stock price should exceed $85 per share at the close of the trading on November 15, 2013, I received a cash "premium" of $7.75 per share for that commitment.

In case you did not notice, the difference between the two illustrations is that in the first illustration, the target-selling price (strike price of $90 per share) is above the purchase price of $88.65 per share. In the second illustration, the target-selling price (strike price of $85 per share) is below the purchase price of $88.65 per share. The reason I received $7.75 instead of $5.05 as a cash premium for selling the covered call that had a target sale price of $85 for each OXY share, is that a portion of the cash premium amount represented $3.65, the amount by which target price of $85 was less than the current purchase price of $88.65 for each OXY share. If you are willing to set a covered call target-selling price below the current stock market price, the least amount you will receive by issuing the covered call is the difference between the two prices. This difference amount of $3.65 is often referred to as the "intrinsic" value of the covered call option. An investor will collect that intrinsic value as part of the cash premium at the time of selling the covered call. Again, this intrinsic value only becomes part of the equation whenever the current stock market price of the stock in question is higher than the target or strike price of the covered call option.

As I've stated earlier, numerous publications will explain further the finer details of stock options contracts, including covered calls. I will also post additional explanatory materials on my website, which you are invited to visit at any time.

Now I will present to you a series of numeric calculations illustrating each of the five possible outcomes I described above. I will do this for both illustrations. The best way to see the differences is to look at each of the five possible outcomes, and compare them to each scenario I will present.

Five possible outcomes of covered call with target price <u>above</u> purchase price:

1)If the price <u>stays the same</u> at $88.65:

-$88.65Purchase price of each share OXY on 6/24/13

+$ 5.05Call option premium received on 6/24/13 to sell OXY at $90

-$83.60Net out-of-pocket cost basis for each share OXY

+$88.65Market value of OXY at the end of day on 11/15/13

+ $ 5.05Net gain if sold at $88.65 per share on next trading day

+ $ 0.64Dividend received on approximately 9/6/13

+ $5.69 Total gain—assume OXY sold for $88.65 a share

$5.69 / $83.60 = 6.8% realized rate of return

2.4 x 6.8% = 16.3% rate of return—annualized (if compounded)

2)If the price goes <u>up by a small amount</u> to $9

-$88.65Purchase price of each share OXY on 6/24/13

+$ 5.05Call option premium received on 6/24/13 to sell OXY at $90

-$83.60Net out-of-pocket cost basis for each share OXY

+$90.00Sale proceeds—if market closing price is $90 on 11/15/13

+ $ 6.40Net gain

+ $ 0.64Dividend received on approximately 9/6/13

+ $7.04 Total gain—assume OXY called away and sold for $90 a share

$7.04 / $83.60 = 8.4% realized rate of return

2.4 x 8.4% = 20.2% rate of return—annualized (if compounded)

3) If the price goes <u>up by a large amount</u> to $100:

-$88.65 Purchase price of each share OXY on 6/24/13

+$ 5.05 Call option premium received on 6/24/13 to sell OXY at $90

-$83.60 Net out-of-pocket cost basis for each share OXY

+$90.00 Sale proceeds—even if market closing price is $100 on 11/15/13

+ $ 6.40 Net gain

+ $ 0.64 Dividend received on approximately 9/6/13

+ $7.04 Total gain—assume OXY called away and sold for $90 a share

$7.04 / $83.60 = 8.4% realized rate of return

2.4 x 8.4% = 20.2% rate of return—annualized (if compounded)

[NOTE: You might think that because the stock price increased to $100 at the time it was sold, that our investor should have a larger gain than shown in the example where the stock was sold at the $90 contract price. The target selling price selected by the investor became a binding contract to sell at $90 per share, in exchange for which the investor received compensation in the form of a premium of $5.05 per share. Whether the market price of the stock is $90 or $100 or $120 or even $200 per share, the covered call options exchange process will automatically sell the shares at $90 per share. The profit does not change no matter how high the stock goes at the contract expiration date, as long as it has reached $90 or higher.]

4)If the price goes <u>down by a small amount</u> to $85:

-$88.65Purchase price of each share OXY on 6/24/13

<u>+$ 5.05</u>Call option premium received on 6/24/13 to sell OXY at $90

-$83.60Net out-of-pocket cost basis for each share OXY

<u>+$85.00</u>Market value of OXY at the end of day on 11/15/13

+ $ 1.40Net gain if sold at $85 per share on next trading day

<u>+ $ 0.64</u>Dividend received approximately 9/6/13

+ $2.04 Total gain—assume OXY was sold for $85 per share

$2.04 / $83.60 = 2.4% realized rate of return

2.4 x 2.4% = 5.9% rate of return—annualized (if compounded)

5)If the price goes <u>down by a large amount</u> to $80:

-$88.65Purchase price of each share OXY on 6/24/13

<u>+$ 5.05</u>Call option premium received on 6/24/13 to sell OXY at $90

-$83.60Net out-of-pocket cost basis for each share OXY

<u>+$80.00</u>Market value of OXY at the end of day on 11/15/13

-$(3.60)Net (loss) if sold at $80 per share on next trading day

<u>+ $ 0.64</u>Dividend received approximately 9/6/13

-$(2.96) Total loss—assume OXY was sold for $80 per share

-$2.96 / $83.60 = -3.5% realized rate of return (negative)

2.4 x -3.5% = -8.5% rate of return (negative)—annualized (if compounded)

In Illustration #6, after looking at all five possible prices of OXY stock on November 15, 2013, we can see that in four of the five possible price outcomes, the investor still makes a positive return. Only when the stock price made a large downward move did the investor lose money. Even in the fifth variation, when the stock price moved downward from $88.65 to $80 per share, a downward movement of about 10%, the actual monetary loss was only 3.5%. By virtue of the cash premium received plus the dividend received, there was partial downside protection. The covered call program in this example eliminated close to two-thirds of the loss suffered by the decline of the stock price. If an investor owned OXY stock in a situation presented in the fifth variation, but without selling a covered call option, the loss endured by such an investor would have been much greater.

This partial loss protection offsets the oft-heard complaint that a covered call program cuts off some of the upside potential. As you could see, in the third variation where the stock price made a large rise, from $88.65 all the way to $100 per share, the commitment when issuing a covered call to sell at $90 per share cut off the last $10 per share of gain. Almost everyone connected with Wall Street would say, and perhaps wisely so, that by employing the covered call strategy, the investor has chosen to sell at a price no greater than $90 per share. Thus, the investor has left $10 of profit or gain on the table, because the stock eventually rose to $100 per share.

I feel I am unique in looking at this situation differently. Let me explain. I feel that the covered call option strategy provides a certain discipline regarding the selection of a target-selling price for your stocks that most individual investors generally do not have. In fact, I believe that many professional institutional investors might not have a consistent selling discipline, either. In many cases where individual investors own stocks, and do not use a covered call strategy, they generally fail to pick a target price at which they would be happy to sell a particular stock held in their portfolio. More significantly, even if an investor had in mind at the time of a stock purchase the ideal price they would be pleased sell that stock, they will invariably change their mind when good luck appears, and the stock price rises to a point at or near that desired price. People get greedy, present company included. Instead of sticking to the discipline of selling at the once-desired target price, people will hang on to see the price go even higher. But stock prices are fickle. In so many cases, the price may stop going up, and slip back down. Then, the person who intended to be so disciplined now hangs on to the stock, trying to "nurse" it back to the previous high price point. Who knows if the stock price will cooperate or not?

The point is that covered call investors are not the only ones who leave gains and profits on the table. I feel justified in stating the opinion that a large percentage of individual investors also erroneously sell their stocks at price points well below the high price points. Many individuals who do not engage in the discipline of a covered call strategy often make matters even worse. Quite often, not having a crystal ball that tells them when a stock reaches its high point, they will watch the very stock that could have been sold for a nice upside gain slide back down near the price they originally paid for it or even lower. In far too many instances, greed trumps discipline.

These undisciplined characteristics probably include most of us, and on many occasions, I've been just as guilty as the next person. With a conservative covered call program, the effort to exercise the discipline of sticking to your target-selling price is mostly eliminated. I'm not suggesting that covered call investors can predict stock prices better than anyone else, or that they necessarily make more money. In simple terms, I have stated the sticking to a discipline with your investments is a powerful tool that is available to all of us. One method of implementing discipline by those of us who find it difficult to do so in a world with so many distractions—from Wall Street and the media—is to use a covered call option investment strategy.

Illustration #7: Covered Call with Target Selling Price <u>Below</u> Purchase Price

I am unique in the world of finance in that I see great value in approaching covered call investing a bit differently than most investment professionals. While most investors use a covered call strategy seeking to sell the underlying stock above the purchase price, I apply the principle of seeking to sell below the purchase price. My rationale is simple: while the opportunity to gain on the upside is more modest, the offsetting benefit of increased downside protection is far greater when targeting to sell below the purchase price. Illustration #7 demonstrates this approach.

Five possible outcomes of covered call with a target price <u>below</u> purchase price:

1) If the price <u>stays the same</u> at $88.65:

-$88.65 Purchase price of each share OXY on 6/24/13

+$ 7.75 Call option premium received on 6/24/13 to sell OXY at $85

-$80.90 Net out-of-pocket cost basis for each share OXY

+$85.00 Sale proceeds—if market closing price is $88.65 on 11/15/13

+$ 4.10 Net gain

+$ 0.64 Dividend received on approximately 9/6/13

+$ 4.74 Total gain—assume OXY called away and sold for $85 a share

$4.74 / $80.90 = 5.9% realized rate of return

2.4 x 5.9% = 14.1% rate of return—annualized (if compounded)

2) If the price goes <u>up by a small amount</u> to $90:

-$88.65 Purchase price of each share OXY on 6/24/13

+$ 7.75 Call option premium received on 6/24/13 to sell OXY at $85

-$80.90 Net out-of-pocket cost basis for each share OXY

+$85.00 Sale proceeds—if market closing price is $90 on 11/15/13

+$ 4.10 Net gain

+$ 0.64 Dividend received on approximately 9/6/13

+$ 4.74 Total gain—assume OXY called away and sold for $85 a share

$4.74 / $80.90 = 5.9% realized rate of return

2.4 x 5.9% = 14.1% rate of return—annualized (if compounded)

3) If the price goes <u>up by a large amount</u> to $100:

-$88.65Purchase price of each share OXY on 6/24/13

+$ 7.75Call option premium received on 6/24/13 to sell OXY at $85

-$80.90Net out-of-pocket cost basis for each share OXY

+$85.00Sale proceeds—if market closing price is $100 on 11/15/13

+$ 4.10Net gain

+$ 0.64Dividend received on approximately 9/6/13

+$ 4.74 Total gain—assume OXY called away and sold for $85 a share

$4.74 / $80.90 = 5.9% realized rate of return

2.4 x 5.9% = 14.1% rate of return—annualized (if compounded)

4)If the price goes <u>down by a small amount</u> to $85:

-$88.65Purchase price of each share OXY on 6/24/13

+$ 7.75Call option premium received on 6/24/13 to sell OXY at $85

-$80.90Net out-of-pocket cost basis for each share OXY

+$85.00Sale proceeds—if market closing price is $90 on 11/15/13

+$ 4.10Net gain

+$ 0.64Dividend received on approximately 9/6/13

+$ 4.74 Total gain—assume OXY called away and sold for $85 a share

$4.74 / $80.90 = 5.9% realized rate of return

2.4 x 5.9% = 14.1% rate of return—annualized (if compounded)

5)If the price goes <u>down by a large amount</u> to $80:

-$88.65 Purchase price of each share OXY on 6/24/13

+$ 7.75 Call option premium received on 6/24/13 to sell OXY at $85

-$80.90 Net out-of-pocket cost basis for each share OXY

+$80.00 Market value of OXY at the end of day on 11/15/13

-$(0.90) Net (loss) if sold at $80 per share on next trading day

+ $ 0.64 Dividend received approximately 9/6/13

-$(0.26) Total loss—assume OXY was sold for $80 per share

-$0.26 / $80.90 = -0.3% realized rate of return (negative)

2.4 x -0.3% = -0.8% rate of return (negative)—annualized (if compounded)

In case you are wondering about losing the difference between the purchase price and the selling price, that amount is generally included in the premium you receive.

I hope you were able to see that once again in the second illustration that in four of the five possible outcomes of the share price of OXY stock, by the time the covered call option expires on November 15, 2013, that the investor will have earned the targeted gain from investing in OXY shares. In this hypothetical illustration, the shares of OXY were purchased for $88.65 per share. Whether the price stays the same, goes up a little, goes up a lot, or goes down a little (not lower than $85 per share), the indicated gain would be $4.74 per share (not factoring in transaction costs or tax effects). Based on my hypothetical assumptions for this second illustration, that covers 80% of the probabilities.

Only in the fifth possible outcome, which might occur with only 20% probability (based on my nonscientific assumptions), would the investor lose money. In this illustration, the downside loss is even less than in the first illustration.

If the stock price falls all the way down to $80 a share by November 15, 2013, the investor who might have used this particular covered call investment would have suffered a loss of only $0.26 per share. This relatively minor loss would compare favorably to other investors who did not employ a covered call strategy. They would have lost something in the area of 9% or 10% in the value of OXY stock—the reduction in stock price from $88.65 down to $80 per share (depending on whether or not the investor collected a dividend of $0.64 per share).

Below I will go through all ten powerful tools of investing to see how many of them are employed in this type of investment strategy, but it's safe to say at the outset that the tool of partial hedging is used in the case of picking a target-selling price below the purchase price of your stock.

I should caution my readers that just as with the shape of snowflakes, no two covered call investments are ever the same. During active stock market trading hours, the prices of stocks and the prices of call options contracts change constantly. The exact combination of stock purchase prices and call option prices rarely, if ever, repeat themselves. Even if they did, an investor could never expect to sit and wait for that event to happen. That is the reason I usually wait until after the markets are closed to gather the last prices of the day, and I know they will remain static overnight or over the weekend until the markets reopen the next trading day. This is not because I expect I will be able to execute trades at those exact closing prices, but rather it allows me to create illustrations of approximations of the rates of return I might be able to receive.

The real rates of return usually turn out relatively close, but they are never the same.

Repeating a final caution to investors, several publications describe a variety of risks connected with trading in both stocks and options contracts that you should obtain from the brokerage firm where you make investments. Even with my hypothetical risk of loss limited to 20% probability, when that probability occurs, losses from stock investing, with and without covered calls, can be substantial.

With the above warnings presented as a reality check, I hope you see the bigger picture in that there are no guaranteed investments in the real world. Reducing your probability of serious losses is the most realistic approach. Think of this as one of always wearing a life vest when on a ship sailing over rough seas, or wearing a parachute when flying solo through stormy skies. It doesn't mean you are safe from all disasters, but you have improved your chances of getting through the deluge safely.

Now let's discuss how many of the ten powerful tools of investing are available to us when using a conservative covered call strategy.

Are All Ten Powerful Tools Used in a Covered Call Strategy?

1) Does It Use the Tool of Compounding?

The illustrations I presented involve setting option expiration dates far enough away in time to at least allow the investor to collect one or more dividend distributions from the company whose stock is purchased. After the call options expire, a stock is either "called" away (sold) or not. In most cases, the dividend payments would have been collected along the way.

No matter what happens, the investor is encouraged to repeat the process in one of two ways. If the stock were sold by being called away, then the investor would take all the proceeds and search for another stock, and repeat the process. Assuming all the proceeds can be reinvested, this invokes the power of compounding. If each expiration period extends for three months, so as to collect dividends four times a year, then the compounding would be on a quarterly basis. However, the call option expiration dates can go out much longer in time, generally as much as a year into the future.

As long as the program continues, there will be compounding, at least annually, or more often than annually. If the program continues for several years, as part of a long-term financial plan, then the power of compounding over time will occur.

2) Does It Use the Tool of Continuous Contributions?

The answer is again yes, and, in fact, it is encouraged. There is every opportunity for an investor who is involved in implementing a financial plan to add money to a covered call program on a regular basis, such as monthly or quarterly. There is a partial limitation on being able to invest smaller amounts, because the requirement regarding call option programs is that stocks must be purchased in 100 share lots to be able to execute the options contracts. So, if the stock you choose to buy is a $50 stock, then each 100 shares cost $5,000. If you can only sock away smaller amounts, such as $500 per month, then it will take ten months of saving to accumulate $5,000. That should not create a problem, because the point of this book is to demonstrate that an effective plan for building your nest egg includes both saving and investing. No matter how long it takes you to accumulate the required amount to make an additional covered call investment, the idea of continuous contributions still applies.

The concept of dollar cost averaging is merely a more structured version of continuous contributions. It certainly applies to a well-managed covered call program.

3) Does It Use the Tool of Habit, Consistency, and Discipline?

In fact, a selling discipline is built into the covered call strategy. Once a price is chosen for a covered call option then that becomes the price that the stock in question will be sold, if the stock rises to that price or higher by the expiration date of the call option contract. If the stock is below the call price at the time of expiration, the investor will have to decide whether to keep the stock, and perhaps sell another call option, or sell the stock and look for another stock in which to invest.

Discipline will also come into play if the stock market is negative and the investor's stock is going down in price. The decision in such instance is no different than owning a stock without a call option program. If the investor has a sell discipline based on a percentage loss, this is going to be the same whether or not a covered call program is implemented.

4) Does It Use the Tool of Limited Diversification?

A covered call program is an excellent example of a strategy that employs the tool of limited diversification. Because option contracts always involve the purchase or sale of 100 share lots, it requires a certain amount of investment capital into each stock that an investor will select. This will generally limit the number of the stocks that a person can invest in, and thus limits the diversification to a practical number of stocks limited to the amount of money in the investment program at any one time.

In addition, a covered call program requires a certain amount of research that will reveal those stocks with the better potential to deliver the desired rates of return in support of the investor's financial plan. This will likewise limit the number of stocks in which to invest. An investor should seek at least two to four stocks in which to invest, but it is not necessary to have that broad of a selection to have a successful covered call program.

5) Does It Use the Tool of Limited Leverage?

Again, the answer is yes. In this instance, it's a bit more subtle, but this tool is employed in a covered call strategy, and in a couple of ways.

Any stock investor can open a brokerage "margin" account. This means the investor can borrow money from the brokerage firm where they do the stock trading. Generally speaking, if a person opens a brokerage account with $50,000, for example, in cash or stock holdings, the person can borrow an additional $50,000 so as to be able to invest in a total of $100,000 in stocks (and related covered calls). However, that would be a risky situation if you borrowed the maximum allowed, because for every dollar your selected stock might go down in value, you would be negative by $2. That's too risky.

If you invest just the cash that you have invested in your brokerage account, without any margin borrowing, there is still a certain amount of "leverage" that takes place with a covered call strategy. You are using a small amount of "other people's money" when you activate a covered call on the stock shares you own. For example, if you buy a stock for $50 per share (in a bundle of 100 shares), the cost would be $5,000. If you then write (meaning "sell" or activate) a covered call on your 100 shares to sell the shares at say $55 per share, you might receive $2 per share as an option "premium" for writing the covered call. In reality, your actual cost per share is only $48.

The reason I call this "limited leverage" is that you are buying a $50 stock for only $48 per share. In our example, the out-of-pocket cost is only $4,800 instead of $5,000. If your stock value rises to $55 per share or higher, then instead of $5 per share profit, you are gaining $7 per share (plus any dividend received, and minus commissions for transaction costs). Although the leverage is small, in this scenario an investor would be increasing a 10% gain ($55 less $50) to a 14% gain ($55 less $48).

If you can repeat this procedure three or four times per year, and factor in the tool of compounding, this investment tool of limited leverage is indeed powerful.

6) Does It Use the Tool of Limited Hedging?

The answer to this is similar to that of limited leverage. For this tool, hedging is really the concept of protecting on the downside. It is important that I be clear to all my readers that whenever you purchase any stock investment, the price of the stock can, and often will, go down from the price you paid for it. If you are not required to sell a stock investment while it is down in price, you can always wait and hope the price eventually increases and goes higher than the price you paid for it.

A hedge is an arrangement that fully or partially protects the investor from losses when values go down. In most cases, hedging arrangements cost money, and some people view such costs as wasted money if the price of their stock never did go down, and, in fact, only went up. Because of the nature of the stock market and the economy, you are never sure if your stock values will go up or go down in the future.

Interestingly enough, a conservative covered call program does provide a small amount of downside protection. That is the reason I feel justified in stating that covered calls employ the tool of limited hedging.

Using the same example of buying 100 shares of stock for $50 per share, and making a commitment to sell the shares for $55 per share by selling a covered call, a limited hedge has been created. If you recall, the investor in this example received a call option premium of $2 per share for committing to sell at $55 per share. As a result, the out-of-pocket cost was really $48 per share. In addition, I'm including in the example that the investor will also receive a dividend payment of $0.50 per share before the call option period expires (whether or not the stock is "called" away at $55 per share).

Since the investor is justified in expecting the receipt of $2.50 per share ($2 of option premium and $0.50 of dividend), the investor will only suffer the risk of a loss if the stock price falls below $47.50 per share. The covered call investor will have $2 more downside protection than the ordinary investor who also paid $50 per share (it is assumed that all investors will receive a $0.50 dividend payment).

In our example, the covered call investor has a partial hedge that is not huge, but at least lets them ride the stock down a little further, and with less worry, than the ordinary investor not using a covered call strategy.

The reason I claim this form of limited hedging as a powerful tool is that even though it offers only partial downside protection, the investor does not have to pay a fee to get a few percentage points of downside protection. On the contrary, the covered call investor gets paid a call option premium for engaging in this partial hedging strategy. If you think about this for a bit, the difference between paying for a hedging strategy and getting paid even a small amount for partial downside protection can add up quickly on an annualized basis.

7) Does It Use the Tool of Low Fees, Commissions, and Taxes?

Investors always have a choice when choosing a brokerage firm for trading stocks and options. Therefore, you can choose an online broker, a discount broker, or one of the major Wall Street full-service brokerage firms depending on your preference. This choice applies whether you are investing in stocks alone, or mutual funds, or bonds, or in our case, a covered call program.

Implementation of a covered call strategy involves trading call options contracts, in addition to buying and selling the stocks in question. As a result, there are extra commissions charged for issuing covered call options contracts. However, since an investor can choose to make trades at discount brokerages, or even online, there are still opportunities to pay lower commissions and fees than those at full-service brokerage firms.

As far as lowering taxes are concerned, it is a bit more difficult to lower the tax impact on gains from a successful covered call program, but it is possible to do so. Firstly, most brokerage firms will allow a covered call strategy to be used in retirement accounts, such as IRA and 401(k) accounts. The outcomes of all trades, including options trades, are tax-free at the time of the transactions. The reason trades in qualified retirement accounts are not subject to taxation is that they are viewed by most Wall Street firms as being very conservative, and therefore suitable for retirement accounts. Only when the investor decides to withdraw distributions from the retirement account itself will the investor pay taxes at their ordinary income tax rate.

Secondly, even if not traded in a retirement account, when stocks are purchased as part of a covered call program and are held for more than a year, the gains on the stock sales can qualify for the lower rates on long-term capital gains. There is even a category of call options contracts that have expiration dates more than a year away that will also qualify for the lower tax rates of long-term gains. These types of call options are generally referred to as LEAPS.

The tool of lower commissions, fees, and taxes is available when investing in a conservative covered call program.

8) Does It Use the Tool of Investing in Stocks from Companies with Strong Financial Statements?

Owning stocks is an integral part of a covered call program and are the underlying securities to the call option strategy. If an investor is going to purchase stocks as part of a saving and investing program, then it makes perfect sense for the investor to select stocks of companies that have a long track record of strong financial statements.

The backbone of American stock exchanges is companies with strong financial statements and innovative products and services that keep our country at the forefront of entrepreneurial progress. Even for those investors who choose bonds as their core investment strategy, strong companies are those who will be able to keep making their interest payments and routinely pay off their debts.

When implementing a covered call strategy, it is my opinion that you are better off choosing a strong financially sound company that has a long history of paying steady dividends. No one can predict price changes in the stock market, but financially sound companies tend to have more stable stock prices than companies who live on their "story" alone. Stable stock prices often lead to more successful returns for those using a covered call strategy.

Companies who do not have excessive debt, and which generate substantial cash year in and year out, are a pretty good bet to keep paying their dividends, and maybe even grow their dividends on a regular basis.

Companies with strong financial statements are available in sufficient abundance, to be selected for implementation of a covered call program.

9 & 10) Does It Use the Tool of Treating Investing Like Running a Business and the Tool of Knowing What You Can and Cannot Control?

This final couple of tools, treating investing like running a business and knowing what you can control and cannot control, can be examined together. The idea of treating your stock investments as if you are running a business is really saying that you should be objective and rational in the handling of your investments. I urge investors to never get emotionally attached to any single stock, and to make investment decisions based on the economic potential of the stock in question.

If you run a retail store and some of your inventory does not sell very well—perhaps it's now out of season—you will unload the slow-moving merchandise at whatever discount it takes to make room for in-season hot sellers. The same should be done with your stocks. If the recent hot stock that you bought has all of a sudden gone out of favor and has dropped in value by 10% or 20%, then unload the stock. Do not make the fatal mistake of saying, "I'll just wait until it comes back to the price I paid for it, then I'm going to sell it."

Seriously, it's the money that is important, not the name of the stock. If your portfolio loses value because a particular stock goes down in value, sell it off at a loss and then put the money that's left into a stock that you determine has a greater probability of going up in value in the near future. Why hang on to the loser that on the surface has the propensity for maybe losing even more? Take that money and put it into a stock with a better track record. Is this a guarantee of absolute certainty you'll make back all your losses? No, of course not. But, my business mind suggests that the better probability of making up the money you lost will be with a stock that has a record of better performance, in relation to the general stock market, then the stock that just lost you 10% or 20% of your investment.

Think like a businessperson, and don't get loyal to any stocks. The stocks themselves do not know if you own their shares, and even if they did, they probably wouldn't even care.

Similarly, with regard to knowing what you can and cannot control in the world of stock investing, this tool is likewise based on the concept of an investor being objective and realistic about their stock investments. You, as an investor, cannot control the stock market, the movement of stock prices, interest rates, the financial markets in Europe, the value of the yen versus the dollar, or nuclear reactor explosions halfway around the world.

What you can control is the amount you contribute each pay period into your IRA fund or to your 401(k) plan. You can control whether you invest in stocks with strong financial statements, or not. You can control whom you hire or fire as your broker or investment advisor. It is my contention that in a majority of instances, the items you can control have a greater impact on the success of your financial plan than do the items you cannot control. In the long run, the amount you continually contribute on a regular basis to your retirement plan has a greater impact on the success of your retirement plan than does the ups and downs of the stock market or the status of the economy in Europe. You can control the amount and frequency of your retirement contributions, but you cannot control interest rates.

Why spend so much time allowing the things you cannot control to distract you, when you might reap far more rewards concentrating and spending time on the things you can control? You can control the selection of your stocks and the target price at which you desire to sell them. Yes, a covered call strategy uses the tools of handling your investments like running a business and of knowing what you can and cannot control.

Themes for Taking Control of Your Financial Future

As we conclude our time together, there are five recurring themes that I've stressed throughout this book that I would like to now summarize. I sincerely hope you will be able to internalize and assimilate these ideas in your effort to avoid the distractions, yet implement the powerful tools Wall Street has to offer.

First, be an investor. Each of us who desires to grow a nest egg for achieving our future financial goals should ask the question, "Am I an investor, or am I a speculator?" The ability to know the difference between an investment as opposed to a speculation or a gamble is presented several times in these pages. As a quick refresher, if you are looking for the price to increase whatever you place your money in, you are a speculator. If you are seeking periodic and recurring cash flow from the purchase of an investment vehicle, then you are an investor. Depending on your approach, the purchase of stocks and bonds can fall into either category. I strongly recommend you work at being an investor.

Second, be a saver. To become successful in reaching your financial goals, I feel that you can greatly improve your odds, no matter the size of your wealth at the beginning of the process, if you add a savings component to your investment program. The idea of being a continuous, diligent saver goes all the way back to the fable of the tortoise and the hare. Plodding along diligently without distractions is not easy, but it can bring surprisingly large rewards. The concept of investing, and even that of speculating, implies a one-time monetary infusion into whatever investment vehicle you feel has great potential. Adding the concept of saving and investing together now involves continuous additions to the implementation of your financial plan. It may be difficult for everyone to find sources from which to make continuous monetary additions to your investments, but if you do so, the probability of success, in the end, is increased exponentially.

Third, know what you can and cannot control. To reduce stress and worry about your investments, I urge you to be aware of the concept of knowing what you can and cannot control during the implementation process of planning for your financial goals. We need to recognize that we cannot control the economy, or the taxation rates, or even the up and down prices of the stocks we buy. Once we recognize this, perhaps we can be more objective about the news we receive on the economy and the markets. If we focus on things we can control, and understand how much those items impact our ultimate success or failure, it should help reduce our stress. We can control the nature of the goals we set. We can control how much we want to save, and how frequently we actually make contributions to our investment accounts.

Once you, the saver-investor, acknowledges what things you can and cannot control, and you focus primarily on what you can control, the stress level should go down. There will be less worry and fewer sleepless nights.

Fourth, don't try to beat the market. The measure of the success of any investment program should never be based on trying to exceed or beat a benchmark rate of return. Just because the Dow Jones Industrial Average or the S&P 500 Index reaches a certain level during the course of a year, it does not dictate the measure of the success of your particular investment program. The outcome of the total return experienced by your favorite benchmark has no bearing on the success or failure of your particular financial plan.

If your plan calls for an average annual rate of return of 6.5%, for example, it is not a failure when the actual benchmark index achieved a 13.5% rate of return for the year. If the reality of your portfolio was an actual return of 7.5% for the year, that is not a failure by 6%. Instead, you exceeded your required rate of return by 1.0%, because all your plan required was a rate of return per year of 6.5%.

Beating benchmark rates of return impose a false standard of success for your financial plan implementation, and we ought to stop doing that. I urge investors to know your investment strategy, determine your required rate of return, and then impose that as the measure of your success.

Fifth, ask and answer the five key questions. If you want to save and build a nest egg for retirement, or for the down payment on a first home or a second home, or to establish a college fund for your children, asking and answering our five basic planning questions will provide a blueprint for your financial plan.

The five key questions are, once again, as follows: 1) How much money do you need to accumulate to achieve this goal? 2) How much money do you have now to begin the implementation of your plan? 3) How many years do you expect it will take to accumulate the desired amount? 4) How much new money do you feel you can contribute (or save) on a regular basis (weekly, monthly, annually), to add to your plan? 5) What annual rate of return (compounded) will be required to allow you to accumulate the amount you desire?

I urge readers to keep in mind, and fully internalize, these five basic themes of this book. I feel that these are different from those of other investment books that deal with Wall Street investing. I feel that constantly attempting to exceed benchmark returns is ultimately a recipe for disaster. Somewhat more subtly speaking, because the desired rate of return for your investment program is usually well below that of a benchmark index, it should be easier to achieve. There should be less stress involved in attempting to achieve a more modest rate of return, and as a result, fewer sleepless nights.

Section 4 Summary

In this section of the book, I endeavored to integrate the concepts from the first three sections into some common themes that would allow you, the reader, to take away some basic principles related to Wall Street investing. Some of the more important themes tied together in this final section were as follows.

Of primary importance is the concept of combining both saving and investing as essential to building a nest egg. Any program for accumulating a financial nest egg, achieved with a minimum of stress, yet with consistency and discipline, requires employing elements of savings and investing working together.

On more than one occasion, I have presented the difference between being an investor as opposed to being a speculator. Only a lucky few, in some cases only those few with an unfair advantage, will generally win at speculation. Whether it comes to playing the lottery, playing at the blackjack table, or picking a daily double at the track, not all who participate can win. When speculating, often more realistically referred to as gambling, those who win do so at the expense of all other participates. In contrast, everyone who has sufficient resources, and participates in a true investment endeavor, can enjoy a certain level of success and positive return on their investment.

I began the process of tying it all together by suggesting to readers, who are seeking to accumulate a nest egg to achieve their financial goals, to ask themselves the following three questions:

What are my financial goals?

Am I implementing my financial plan in a productive and disciplined manner?

Am I achieving an average compounded rate of return on my investments that is consistent with achieving the desired growth of my nest egg?

The next important theme in building a nest egg, for any purpose, involves combining both saving and investing. One without the other does not maximize the potential of the two processes combined. Grandma on the farm knew how to save, and she was very successful in so doing. We can learn a lot from Grandma's discipline and consistency. But no one ever taught her how to invest, even modestly. So she missed the opportunity to increase the size of her nest egg beyond the amounts that she socked away. She was never blessed with the benefits of the powerful tool of compounding.

In this section, we also discussed the types of accounts and methods of holding your assets. This is a matter of knowing where your money is and what it is doing. These accounts and methods include:

- The Cookie Jar and Under the Mattress

- Brokerage Accounts and Bank Accounts

- Various Types of Retirement Accounts: 401(k)s, IRAs, and Pensions

- Trusts and Estates

- Fee-based Registered Investment Advisory Firms

We next discussed specific types of investments to potentially make your money grow. We focused on five categories that have historically shown a promising rate of return. The goal was to introduce and define these investment options and help you gain a better understanding of what might work best for you. These types of investments include:

- Real Estate

- Stock Investments

- Bonds and Fixed Income Investments

- Life Insurance and Annuities

- Illustrations Using Ten Powerful Tools

The most important goal of this book is to educate and empower you to feel more in control, and less stressed about your financial goals and financial future. As the ten powerful tools were identified specifically for this reason, it is only fitting that we apply them in a practical fashion. As one of my areas of expertise is covered calls, we applied the ten powerful tools to two different covered call strategies.

Lastly, as this book is about demystifying the saving and investing process, we concluded with the five core questions as they apply to the accumulation phase and the spending phase.

AFTERWORD

I want to thank you for taking this journey with me. I want to applaud you for taking the time to become better informed. I want to encourage you to continue the process of planning for your financial future, and more importantly, toward implementing the plan you've created that will hopefully achieve your financial goals. I plan to continue to make developments in the area of minimizing the distractions of Wall Street, and knowing what you can and cannot control in dealing with the economy. Please visit my website for more information: www.customizewallstreet.com.

I hope you will be able to easily decide if you are an investor or a speculator, and then choose which you want to be. Only a lucky few can win at speculating, whereas those who wish to participate responsibly can be successful with their investments.

I have tried to guide you in the direction of combining a plan for continuous saving with a plan for sensible investing. I see huge benefits in such an approach. Hopefully, you will see it too.

It is my desire that you learn to disregard the numerous distractions of Wall Street, especially the implied allegation that the only measure of success is that of beating the so-called benchmark index, whatever that benchmark might be.

I hope you learn that any financial goal or plan that can be measured in dollars requires the asking and answering of five key numerical questions. You have the power to control and modify the answer to four of those questions, based on your economic reality. These questions will naturally allow you to self-assess the reasonableness of your goals and plan and allow you the ability to make necessary adjustments. The answer to the fifth question is simply a plug figure that you calculate.

Wall Street makes available some wonderful tools for successful investing, ten of which I expanded upon in this book. I hope you will become comfortable using some or all of them, knowing you can control them, and you can use them without stress, worry, or anxiety.

I strongly feel the main reason any of us should use Wall Street, and its wonderful tools for saving and investing, is to plan for and to implement whatever our personal financial goals might be.

It is only when we have no long-range purpose or plan for our savings or investing dollars—and allow ourselves to be distracted by the unnecessary agendas of Wall Street and media advertising—that we often just spin our wheels. Saving and investing should have a goal and a purpose. If not, why use Wall Street? Casinos can be a lot more entertaining.

ACKNOWLEDGEMENTS

While this book is the reflection of decades of my personal experience, it is also a reflection of direct and indirect contributions from many people. I would like to personally acknowledge the following people:

The late Dale Fetherling, who gave me the initial direction and impetus to get this book published.

Antoinette Kuritz and the La Jolla Writers Conference faculty for providing incredible information. A special thanks to author and LJWC faculty member, Jesse Kellerman, for showing genuine interest and encouragement.

Jeniffer Thompson and the Monkey C Media team for their creativity and ingenuity in the interior and cover design of this book, and for the design of my website.

Jeff Provence of Premier Fund Solutions, who provided me with the opportunity to pursue the world of Wall Street mutual fund portfolio management—Southern California Style.

Jared Kuritz of STRATEGIES PR for his friendship and professionalism, believing in me as a writer, providing me with unfettered patience and support, and for shepherding this project from partial manuscript to published book.

My son and daughter-in-law, Dan and Lauren, and my daughter, Shelley, who continually inspire me to try to be a good father.

ABOUT THE AUTHOR

Harvey Neiman earned his bachelor's degree in Political Science from U.C. Santa Barbara, his JD degree at the University of San Diego School of Law, and later earned an LLM degree in Taxation, also at USD School of Law.

He has had a versatile career in both law and portfolio investment management. He was a professor of law for more than 15 years, at Thomas Jefferson School of Law in San Diego, California, having taught such varied courses as Constitutional Law, Community Property, Taxation, and Estate Planning. Later, he trained for a new career, and thereafter served as an account executive in the world of stock investments at Merrill Lynch, and later at Morgan Stanley, both in La Jolla, Calif.

Subsequently, he launched his investment advisory firm, with his son Daniel. Father and son are the lead principals of Neiman Funds, a mutual fund family they launched in 2003. Harvey serves as President and Chief Investment Officer of Neiman Funds Management LLC based in upstate New York.

Harvey works from his home in Rancho Santa Fe, Calif. He plays beach volleyball in the summer, snowboards in the winter, and plays tennis and golf year round.